D1418114

Truth from Trash

Truth from Trash
How Learning Makes Sense

Chris Thornton

The MIT Press
Cambridge, Massachusetts
London, England

© 2000 Massachusetts Institute of Technology

This book was set in Sabon by Asco Typesetters, Hong Kong, and was printed and bound in the United States of America.

Library of Congress Cataloging-in-Publication Data

Thornton, Christopher James.
 Truth from trash: how learning makes sense / Chris Thornton.
   p.   cm. — (Complex adaptive systems)
 Includes bibliographical references and index.
 ISBN 0-262-20127-5 (hc.: alk. paper)
 1. Machine learning. I. Title. II. Series.
Q325.4.T47   2000
006.3′1—dc21   99-16505
                                                        CIP

Contents

Preface

Commander Data, The Borg, Nanites, Daleks, Cybermen, K9, Gort, Hal, Holly, Kryten, Huey, Duey, Luey, Marvin the Paranoid Android, Metal Mickey, R2D2, C3PO, Robocop, Robbie the Robot, Terminator, Tweaky....

Robots. The movies are full of them. But in real life, they are scarce to the point of virtual nonexistence. At your local shopping center you are unlikely to be able to buy a decent sandwich-making robot regardless of the amount of money you are prepared to spend. And the same goes for robotic chauffeurs, robotic bed-makers, robotic gardeners, robotic chefs, robotic launderers, robotic counselors, and robotic teachers. We love the *idea* of robots. We would surely buy useful domestic robots in droves if we had the chance. But they are simply *not there*. They are not for sale. They do not exist.

Why is this? Why, at the end of the hi-tech twentieth century, after the investment of space-program-sized wads of cash, are there no useful domestic robots on the market? The truth of the matter is that, at present, no one has a really good answer. But despite the lack of "product," there is no shortage of energy or inventiveness. Rather, the reverse. The mismatch between the fabulous level of investment and the paltry level of return has created a tension among robot workers—a desire to break the mold and branch out in a new directions. The net effect is an adventure culture, an ongoing explosion of variety, upheaval, and reformulation. Sandwich-making robots may be noticeable by their absence, but the outpouring of imaginative robotics-related work is wondrous to behold.

In keeping with the technicolour spirit of the times, this book offers a modestly adventurous view of an issue that is at the core of robotics work: learning. It argues that the process we think of as learning divides into two utterly different processes, one of which is both more challenging (from the engineering point of view) and more cognitively fertile than its counterpart. It goes on to argue that this more sophisticated form of learning involves representation construction and establishes the preconditions for creative activity. More contentiously, the book proposes that creativity may be viewed as a kind of overstimulated learning process.

The adventurous argument has an adventurous methodology to go with it. At heart, the book is a research monograph because it sets out an original thesis with associated arguments and data. But it tries to steer away from the mind-numbing path typically trodden by such works by importing various devices from the pop-science genre. Key background material relating to contemporary learning models is presented in an easy-to-digest form with extensive use of mental imagery and a bare minimum of mathematics. Light relief is injected on a regular basis through a concoction of dialogues, anecdotes, and other forms of non-scientific material. The ultimate aim of the book might be described—to borrow a computer software term—as "edutainment."

Thanks are due to IMSS Firenze for permission to use the images of Johannes Kepler and Tycho Brahe that appear in chapter 3; to Norman Longmate for permission to use the image of Coventry that appears in chapter 6; to Heffers of Cambridge for permission to use the image of Alan Turing that appears in chapter 6; to Andrew Hodges for permission to use the image of the Crown Inn that appears in chapter 6. I would also like to thank Dave Cliff, Andy Clark, Inman Harvey, Jim Stone, Donald Peterson, Ruth Marchant, and Guy Scott for providing one sort of inspiration or another. The deficiencies of the book remain, of course, entirely my own work. Finally, my thanks to James and Amelia for showing me something new (although not necessarily true) about the ways in which trash may be created.

Truth from Trash

1

The Machine That Could Learn Anything

A highlight of the eighteenth SPWBA conference was "The Machine That Can Learn Anything." Devised by the succinctly named "Professor A.," this exhibit drew attention from a broad cross section of delegates. Its success appears to have been partly due to its striking visual appearance. While other exhibits sported the chromium hi-tech look, the "Machine That Can Learn Anything" offered something more primitive. A small, black tent adorned with astrological motifs, relieved by the color screen of a laptop just visible through a velvet-edged opening. On the outside of the tent, a handwritten sheet welcomed visitors and encouraged them to submit trial learning tasks to the machine. Instructions at the end of the sheet specified the terms of engagement. "Tasks must be presented in the form of example association pairs," it asserted. "The machine can then be tested by presentation of test items. A task will be considered to have been successfully learned if the machine is able to produce correct associations for test items in the majority of cases."

Visitors wishing to test the machine's ability had thus to express learning tasks in the form of association pairs. Let's say the visitor wished to test machine's ability to learn addition. He or she had first to write down a list of suitably representative associations. For example:

```
1 1 -> 2
1 2 -> 3
2 5 -> 7
4 2 -> 6
8 1 -> 9
```

This list had then to be presented to the machine via its "sensory organ": a hole in the tent's rear panel. Having passed in their list of associations, testers had then to move around to the screen at the front of the tent and wait until such time as the machine printed out an instruction inviting the submission of a query. Testers could then type in items and evaluate the machine's responses (suggested associations) as correct or incorrect. At each stage the machine would present performance statistics, that is, show the proportion of test items upon which correct associations had been generated. And without exception, testers found that the machine performed in an exemplary fashion. It was, indeed, able to generate correct associations in the majority of cases.

Many visitors were visibly impressed by the behavior of the machine. Some were inclined to reserve judgment; a few showed complete disinterest. But from the practical point of view, the exhibit was a runaway success. In addition to hosting an estimated 2000 visitors in less than a week, it was the recipient of a quite unexpected level of media attention. The day after opening, a national newspaper printed a 1000-word report on Professor A.'s work under the banner headline "Learn-Anything Machine Is a Labour of Love." And on the final two days of the exhibition, no fewer than three TV stations ran news items covering the exhibit itself. The media take on A.'s machine was unanimously upbeat, and commentators were uncharacteristically supportive. In just a few years' time, one suggested, members of the public could expect to be "teaching" their computers to do things rather than laboriously "commanding" them using the mouse and keyboard.

When asked how the machine worked, Professor A. noted there was no magic involved; the machine simply applied well-known techniques from the field of *machine learning*, a subfield of computer science concerned with intelligent computers. But he admitted that the role played by the machine's "sensory organ" was significant. "The key to the machine's success," he noted, "is that users can only present learning tasks in a particular way, namely as association or prediction tasks. This is the format assumed by many methods in machine learning. By forcing users to present their problems this way, we open up the whole repertoire of machine learning methods. We make it possible to employ any method we like on any problem we're presented with."

With his bold rhetoric, Professor A. quickly swayed the media to his side. But the academic rank and file were less easily persuaded. As the conference neared a conclusion, grassroots opinion turned against Professor A., and at a plenary session held on the final day, his machine became the focus of a rising tide of hostile attention. One critic suggested that rather than being able to "learn anything," A.'s machine was actually limited to the solving of formally specified prediction problems. Another argued that since the machine had no way of actively interacting with the world, there was no basis upon which it could carry out *any* sort of cognitive activity, let alone learning.

Professor A. remained unmoved. He accepted the proposition that the machine's abilities involved prediction. But, somewhat to the surprise of his detractors, he rejected the idea that there was any real difference between this task and that of learning. He then went on to challenge the audience to come up with a learning problem that could *not* be interpreted as a type of prediction problem.

The assembly was temporarily silenced. Then a shout rang out. "What about concept learning?" demanded a man standing at the very rear of the hall. Professor A. contemplated the question for a moment and then moved cautiously toward the overhead projector. "OK. But let us pretend that I have never heard of concept learning," he said, taking a green felt-tip from his pocket. "Now you tell me how you would like to specify a concept learning problem."

The man thought for a few moments before responding. "Something that can do concept learning obviously has to be able to acquire the ability to distinguish between things which are part of the concept and things which are not part of the concept."

"Fine," said A. "And how should we specify this result?"

The man sensed that the question was intended to snare him. But he was unable to prevent himself from falling into the professor's trap. In attempting to provide a formal specification for a concept learning problem, the man found himself beginning to talk in terms of a *mapping* between certain situations and certain responses.

"But this mapping you are describing can also be viewed as specifying a prediction problem, can it not?" replied the professor when the man finally come to a stop. No answer was forthcoming. The professor continued to his punch line. "And this is exactly the format which is required by my machine, yes? So we find that in formally specifying a learning problem we inevitably produce something which can be interpreted as a prediction problem. One has to conclude there is no *formal* difference between the two types of tasks."

It was a well-rehearsed performance. But still, many members of the audience remained unconvinced. Some went so far as to offer further responses to the "challenge." The professor was thus given the opportunity to demonstrate by similar reasoning that several other forms of learning—including skill acquisition, function learning, language development, classification learning, and behavior learning—were all equivalent, under formal specification, to the task of prediction. When it became obvious that there was no mileage to be gained on this territory, the flow of criticism began to dry up. One hardy individual, however, refused to give in.

"It amazes me," he commented bluntly, "that anyone could think that prediction and learning were the same thing. Surely it is obvious that many natural organisms do the latter but not the former."

"Well, that may be," agreed the professor. "But so what? I never claimed that prediction and learning are the same thing. The processes may be—probably are—quite different. What I showed was that specifications of learning tasks are always equivalent to specifications for prediction tasks. So the tasks have to be the same. Even if the solutions are different."

"But aren't you just making a theoretical distinction?" responded the truculent delegate. "Most interesting learning tasks can't be given formal specifications in advance. So the real issue is how a learning agent can develop behavior that doesn't have a neat, formal specification."

The professor nodded, considering (or pretending to consider) the point at length. "Well, I'm not sure that it makes sense to say you have a learning task if you cannot formally specify what that task is. That seems to me to be a contradiction. And changing the topic to behavior learning makes no difference. Either there is a behavior or there is not a behavior. And if there is, it must be possible, at least in principle, to say *what* that behavior is, that is, to give it a formal specification. I cannot see how we can escape this. I really can't. So it seems to me unavoidable that I have been right all along."

1.1 Back to Reality

So much for the story of Professor A. What are *we* to make of the Machine That Can Learn Anything? How should we interpret the professor's immodest defense at the plenary session? Is the machine itself some sort of fake? Are the professor's arguments about the formal equivalence of learning tasks and prediction tasks mere sophistry? The reader will probably have formed an opinion. But the line pursued in this book will be essentially *pro*. That is to say, it will tend to go along with the argument that learning can be treated as an attempt to solve a prediction task. The idea sounds implausible—even absurd—at first hearing. But it becomes more digestible with familiarity.

Any dictionary definition will confirm that learning involves the acquisition of knowledge or behavior. But since knowledge acquisition can always be viewed as the learning of new "conceptual behavior," we can justifiably treat *all* learning as some form of behavior learning. This simplifies things considerably. But we can go a stage further.

A complete specification of a behavior must show how it involves the production of certain actions in certain situations. So whenever we attempt to fully specify a learning task, we must identify the relevant associations between situations and actions. But as soon as we do this, we are caught on the professor's hook. Our problem specification defines the task in terms of a *mapping*. We can always read this mapping in two ways: as saying what actions should be produced in a given situation or as *predicting* which actions should be produced in a given situation. The two readings are essentially equivalent. It does not make any difference if we treat the mapping as specifying a prediction task or a learning task.

Professor A. is thus right in claiming that learning tasks and prediction tasks are equivalent. But what of his claim that his machine can learn *anything*? The professor's argument rests on the fact that he can get his machine to produce above-chance performance on any prediction problem. But does this prove anything? Can it really support the claim that the machine can perform universal learning? To get a better handle on these questions, we need to take a closer look at the process of prediction. We need to see what it involves and what sort of performance is generally achievable.

1.2 Prediction Games

A prediction task stripped to the bones is really just a type of guessing game. It is a contest in which an individual is given some information on a topic, and is then asked to guess information that has been held back. The game of "battleships" is a good example. In this game, two users provide information about their battleship formation on a turn-by-turn basis. The aim of the game is to sink the other person's ships. This involves guessing the locations of the opponent's ships from the information given.

Another common guessing game is that of *sequence prediction*. In this problem a string of numbers is given, and the task is to continue the sequence, that is, to make predictions about numbers that appear later on. For instance, if we are given the sequence

2, 4, 6, 8

and asked to predict the next number, we may well guess

10,

on the grounds that the numbers are increasing by values of 2. However, if we are asked to continue the sequence

2, 4, 6, 8, 10, 13, 16, 19,

we may guess that the next number is 22, or perhaps 23.

Of course, the data presented in prediction problems may be symbolic rather than numeric. They also may take the form of an unordered set rather than a sequence. For example, we might be presented with the data

orange, banana, pear

and asked to predict another item in the same set. A plausible response might be "apple" or "grape." Similarly, a likely guess regarding

Toyota, Ford, Mercedes, VW

might be Datsun.

A scenario that is particular interesting for present purposes occurs when the data are structured objects. For example, let us say we are given the following set of triples

$\langle 1, 4, 4 \rangle, \langle 8, 4, 1 \rangle, \langle 2, 6, 1 \rangle, \langle 3, 3, 3 \rangle, \langle 4, 2, 2 \rangle$

and asked to guess another member of the same set. A plausible guess would be

$\langle 9, 1, 3 \rangle$,

on the grounds that in all the examples, the largest value in the triple is perfectly divisible by both other values. Of course, there may be other plausible rules.

In a variation on the structured data theme, the aim is to predict missing values within *partially* complete data. For example, the task might involve using the examples

$\langle 1, 4, 4 \rangle, \langle 8, 0, 1 \rangle, \langle 2, 6, 1 \rangle, \langle 3, 3, 3 \rangle, \langle 4, 2, 2 \rangle$

to fill in the missing values in

$\langle 6, ?, 1 \rangle, \langle 4, ?, ? \rangle$.

This actually brings us back to the data format required by Professor A. Examples had to be presented to his machine in the form of association pairs, that is, as objects consisting of a set of input values and an associated output. For example,

```
1 1 -> 2
1 2 -> 3
2 5 -> 7.
```

Such data are really just structured objects with an implicit partition between the input values and the output values. The examples above might have been written

```
<1 1 2>
<1 2 3>
<2 5 7>,
```

with the assumption being that the first two values in each object are the given data and the final value is the answer. Correctly formatted test cases could then be written as partially complete triples, such as

```
<3 2 ?>
<4 1 ?>.
```

1.3   Supervised Learning

Prediction tasks presented using Professor A.'s association format are termed *supervised learning* tasks, on the grounds that the examples are like information given to the learner by a teacher or supervisor. When this terminology is used, the thing that is learned is generally termed the *target function*, and the inputs and associated outputs are treated as the arguments and values (respectively) of an unknown function. The learning is then conceptualized along computational lines. The given data (to the left of the arrow) are viewed as *input values*, and the to-be-predicted data (to the right) as *output values*. The learning process is then naturally viewed as the process of acquiring the ability to *compute* the target function.

Input values typically represent the attributes of an object or class. For example, in the association

```
red round smooth -> tasty
```

"red," "round," and "shiny" might be the color, shape, and texture attributes for a particular item (or class) of fruit. In such cases it is natural to view each set of input values as a description of an object written in terms of *variables*. A distinction may then be made between *input variables* and *output variables*, the former being placeholders for the input values and the latter being placeholders for the output values. Further, there is the obvious shortcut in which we refer to a complete set of input values simply as an *input* and a complete set of output values as an *output*. These conventions are illustrated in figure 1.1.

The supervised learning paradigm provides a convenient way of packaging learning problems. But, appearances to the contrary, it does *not* not impose any restrictions or constraints. As the fictional Professor A. demonstrates in the story above, an association-mapping specification merely "fixes the goalposts." It is a specification of the *task* rather than

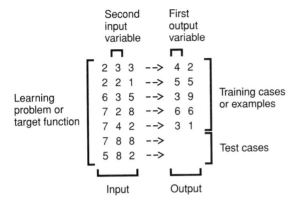

Figure 1.1
Supervised-learning terminology

the *solution*, and thus is completely neutral with respect to the way in which a particular problem may be solved.

1.4 Concept and Classification Learning

Although work in machine learning concerns itself primarily with supervised learning (prediction) tasks, researchers have focused on a number of variations. Attention has been given particularly to the so-called *concept learning problem*. This problem has the same form as the standard supervised learning problem except that target outputs are either "yes" or "no" (sometimes written + and −). Inputs that map onto "yes" are treated as positive examples of a particular concept. Inputs that map onto "no" are treated as negative examples (i.e., counterexamples). And the process of finding a solution to such a problem is then naturally viewed as the process of acquiring the relevant concept.

A sample concept learning problem appears in figure 1.2.[1] Here the inputs are lists of attributes for items of fruit, and the concept is that of edible fruit. Solving this problem can be viewed as the acquisition of the "edible-fruit" concept. Once the problem has been solved, it should be possible to classify test data, that is, novel items of fruit, as either edible or nonedible.

A variation on the theme of concept learning is the *classification problem*. This is just like the concept learning problem except for the fact

```
hairy  brown large hard --> no
smooth green small hard --> yes
hairy  red   small soft --> no
smooth red   large soft --> yes
smooth brown large hard -->
```

Figure 1.2
Edible-fruit concept learning problem

```
gasoline hatchback    FW-drive --> Ford
gasoline convertible  FW-drive --> Ferrari
diesel   saloon       FW-drive --> Ford
gasoline hardtop      RW-drive --> Ferrari
diesel   hardtop      FW-drive -->
```

Figure 1.3
Car classification problem

that we now have a number of target outputs that are the labels of classes. The cases illustrate what sort of object belongs in which class. A sample problem involving the classification of cars appears in figure 1.3. (The variables here describe—working left to right—the fuel used, the body style, and the location of the drive wheels.)

In another version of the supervised learning problem, the inputs take the form of sets of truth-values, with "true" written as 1 and "false" as 0. The aim is to correctly learn the truth function exemplified by the examples. A sample problem appears in figure 1.4.

1.5   Behavior Learning

The supervised learning scenario also lends itself to the problem of *behavior learning*. For example, imagine that we have a simple two-wheeled mobile robot (a "mobot"), circular in shape and with two light sensors on its leading edge, as in figure 1.5(a). Imagine we would like the mobot to use a supervised learning method to learn how to steer away from sources of bright light, as illustrated in the plan diagram of figure 1.5(c) We might proceed by constructing a training set of examples in which each input is a combination of light-sensor values and each output

```
1 1 0 1 1 --> 1

1 0 0 0 0 --> 0

0 1 1 1 0 --> 1

1 1 0 0 1 --> 0

0 0 0 0 0 -->
```

Figure 1.4
Truth-function learning problem

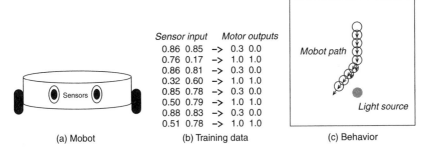

	Sensor input	Motor outputs	
	0.86 0.85	->	0.3 0.0
	0.76 0.17	->	1.0 1.0
	0.86 0.81	->	0.3 0.0
	0.32 0.60	->	1.0 1.0
	0.85 0.78	->	0.3 0.0
	0.50 0.79	->	1.0 1.0
	0.88 0.83	->	0.3 0.0
	0.51 0.78	->	1.0 1.0

(a) Mobot   (b) Training data   (c) Behavior

Figure 1.5
Learning light avoidance

is the combination of signals to be sent to the wheel motors. If the light sensors return higher values for stronger sources of light, and the motors produce an amount of wheel rotation proportional to the relevant signal, then a subset of the input/output pairs might be as shown in figure 1.5(b). The data exemplify the fact that rotational moves (achieved by turning the left wheel only) should be executed whenever either of the input signals exceeds a certain threshold.

If we equip the mobot with supervised learning capability and have it process the data in figure 1.5, then the result should be that the mobot acquires the ability to respond in the desired fashion with respect to sources of light.

1.6 Financial Prediction

One of the most intriguing supervised learning scenarios involves prediction of financial data, such as prices of stocks, bonds, and other

Price of x	Price of y		Future price of z
0.979248	0.058547	-->	0.057332
0.178428	0.784546	-->	0.139985
0.103902	0.024725	-->	0.002569
0.268517	0.639011	-->	0.171585
0.495132	0.159034	-->	

Figure 1.6
Financial prediction problem

commodities. In this variant, the values of the variables are numeric. The input values are given financial data (i.e., current prices of given commodities) and the outputs are to-be-predicted financial data (e.g., the *future* price of some commodity). An illustrative set of data is shown in figure 1.6.

Finding a good solution to this sort of problem might enable us to make money, since it would provide the means of accurately predicting prices from current prices. Imagine that the output values in this mapping are wheat prices and that the application of a learning method to the data produces an input/output rule which, when applied to current prices, suggests that the price of wheat is about to increase. The implication is clear: if we buy wheat stocks now, we should realize a quick profit by selling after the price has risen.

1.7   Learning Problems to Solve by Hand

The best way to come to grips with what supervised learning is all about is to try to *do* it, that is, try to solve some nontrivial, supervised learning problems by hand. The three problems presented below may be used for this purpose. All follow the concept learning model, that is, they all take the form of an input/output mapping in which there are just two distinct outputs. And they all involve a manageably small amount of data, less than one page of input/output pairs. The first problem involves predicting the results of football games. The second involves distinguishing phrases with a certain linguistic property. The third involves deriving a plausible interpretation for a set of card game rules.

Problem 1: Predicting the Football Results

Careful investigation of the football results over a number of weeks shows that the performance of team X can be predicted on the basis of the results for teams A, B, C, D, and E. Thus, it is possible to predict whether X will win or lose just by looking at the results for A, B, C, D, and E. (It is assumed that X never plays A, B, C, D, or E.)

The data set below presents the results for teams A, B, C, D, E, and X recorded over 16 consecutive weeks. Each line shows the results for a particular week. The five input variables represent—working left to right—the results for teams A, B, C, D, and E, and the single output variable represents the result for team X. In all cases, 1 signifies "win" and 0 signifies "lose." The problem is to use the 16 examples to derive the rule that allows team X's result to be predicted from the other teams' results.

```
1 0 0 0 0 --> 0
0 0 0 0 1 --> 0
1 0 1 1 1 --> 1
1 0 1 0 1 --> 0
0 0 1 0 0 --> 0
1 0 0 1 0 --> 1
1 1 1 0 0 --> 1
0 0 0 0 0 --> 0
1 1 1 1 1 --> 1
1 0 1 1 0 --> 1
1 0 0 1 1 --> 1
1 0 0 0 1 --> 0
1 0 1 0 0 --> 0
1 1 1 1 0 --> 1
1 1 1 0 1 --> 1
0 1 1 0 0 --> 1
0 1 1 1 0 -->
1 1 0 1 1 -->
0 1 1 0 1 -->
0 0 1 1 0 -->
```

Problem 2: The Incoherent Tutor

A student takes a course titled "The Production of Coherent Nonsense." Her tutor's method is to present his students with examples of good practice. In one session he takes a set of examples of three-word nonsense phrases and shows which of them should be classified as coherent and which as incoherent. The examples are shown below. The question is, What rule is the tutor using to classify the examples?

```
eypnv gdukk kaqpi --> coherent
psgdr gbaiz htyls --> incoherent
ihytw xbfkg yxcxw --> coherent
panct jlege kkirg --> incoherent
qpcrz vyqkr ygawe --> coherent
ahvlh xggcz nsgff --> incoherent
urmle zybyx gxslm --> incoherent
mbrfc plpkp rojva --> coherent
gdzxa vvjre ztdyj --> coherent
qpmuu begvu rmukx --> incoherent
riijf xdvxm xegum --> coherent
qpheq udrrw zguei --> coherent
qbiha zitck yegyx --> incoherent
sjvva ribyr qqeku --> incoherent
qcsgu qterv hulmf --> incoherent
duzsr rpjao zhmds --> coherent
iruih rxjaw xkgjn --> coherent
fppen mdasf wvfmj --> coherent
eatwk semqd cqewc --> incoherent
cnzbt ilzvl zzmkl --> coherent
hygtt xscza hiijl -->
xibkd uxgzl opcmf -->
eppps bbvtz zggil -->
lhwnu kltla kwzmg -->
```

Problem 3: The Card Player

One evening, a man wandered into town and bought himself a beer in the local saloon. While he drank his beer, he studied a group of settlers gathered around a large table. The settlers appeared to be engaged in some sort of trading activity involving the exchange of small, rectangular cards. The man had no idea what the basis of this activity was. But, being bold, he strode across the room and sat down at the table. The settler immediately to his left nodded to him and began scribbling numbers on a sheet of paper. When he had filled the entire sheet, he pushed it across the table, saying, "If you want to play, you'd better learn the rules." The numbers on the sheet of paper were as shown below. How should they be interpreted? And what rule allows one to predict output values correctly?

```
13  1 9   4 12 1 9   1 9   4 --> 4
2   2 9   1 2  2 9   2 2   2 --> 5
13  3 4   1 11 4 11  4 11  1 --> 4
3   3 12  3 6  3 13  3 1   3 --> 6
2   1 2   1 2  4 12  1 2   2 --> 9
8   3 8   2 8  2 8   4 7   1 --> 9
4   4 4   2 4  4 5   2 4   1 --> 9
7   4 7   4 5  4 5   2 5   4 --> 5
6   4 12  1 6  1 6   4 9   1 --> 4
4   4 9   2 9  4 4   1 4   2 --> 5
6   4 10  4 13 4 9   4 8   4 --> 6
11  1 11  4 11 2 8   3 11  1 --> 9
4   1 7   1 5  1 1   1 13  1 --> 6
10  4 2   3 12 4 12  3 12  2 -->
5   1 7   1 1  1 13  1 4   1 -->
13  2 5   2 13 4 10  1 13  1 -->
```

1.8   A Reasonable Learning Criterion

To conclude the chapter, let us return once more to Professor A. and the Machine That Can Learn Anything. We obviously would like to know whether the machine really does what it is supposed to do, or whether there is some kind of trickery going on. The professor's arguments with respect to the formal equivalence of prediction tasks and learning tasks are sound. Thus we know that any attempt to discredit the machine on the basis of its input limitations fails. But does this mean we have to accept the professor's claims as stated?

The answer is No! Of course the ability to "learn anything" sounds impressive. But when we look carefully at what is really being offered, we find that what you see is not quite what you get. Recall that, according to the rules of engagement, the machine is to be deemed as having success-fully learned the task presented, provided it gets the answers right in the *majority* of cases. This means it can get 49% of the associations wrong and still end up counting itself a winner! Some mistake, surely.

Undoubtedly, Professor A. is conning his audience. But the con has nothing to do with the restricted task presentation format. It has to do with the success criterion that is applied to the learning. When we read the phrase "the majority of cases," we tend to think in terms of figures like 80% or 90%. And, for the unwary, it may therefore sound perfectly reasonable that the machine should be deemed to have successfully learned something provided it produces appropriate answers in the majority of cases. But the criterion is too weak. We would never deem a person to have successfully learned something were he or she to produce inappropriate results in up to 49.99999% of cases. A.'s machine should be treated the same way. The Machine That Can Learn Anything thus has to be considered a fake, pending the introduction of a more restric-tive success criterion.

1.9   Note

1. Note that this and the other "sample problems" in this chapter are merely illustrations. In practice, problems involve a much larger number of associations.

2

Consider Thy Neighbor

Question: Why didn't Intel call the Pentium the 586?
Answer: Because they added 486 and 100 and got 585.999983605.

This well-known joke pokes fun at the Intel Corporation, manufacturer of the x86 chips currently used inside PCs. The initial version of the Pentium chip—replacement for the 486—contained an error that caused some mathematical operations to be computed incorrectly. The error took some time to come to light, and when it did, Intel tried to play down its significance. But the attempt was largely unsuccessful, and widespread publicity ensued. One unnamed source in the American Democratic party even claimed that the landslide Republican victory of November 1994 may have been the result of incorrect computations performed by Pentium CPUs.

In January 1995, a news-group contributor operating under the pseudonym Michel[1] posted an article on-line (in alt.prophecies.nostradamus) that claimed the scandal of the Pentium bug had, in fact, been predicted by Nostradamus in the 16th century. Michel suggests that the prediction is given in *Centuries* 2, quatrain VI.

Aupres des portes & dedans deux citez
Seront deux fleaux, & onc n'apperceut VN TEL,
Faim, dedans peste, de fer hors gens boutez,
Crier secours au grand Dieu immortel.

This may be translated into English as follows:

Near the gates and inside two cities
Will be TWO FLAWS, and nobody noticed it [from] INTEL,
Hunger, pest inside, by steel people thrown out,
Cry for help to the great immortal God.

Michel suggests that "gates" may be a sly reference to Bill Gates, chief of Microsoft, or perhaps to the logic gates of the Pentium microprocessor. The reference to Hunger is an identification of Intel's "greed, which made them hide the flaw and minimize it later." "Pest inside" is Nostradamus's version of the "Intel Inside" campaign slogan. And "by steel" is a cunning reference to the fact that the error involves hardware rather than software. Michel notes that Nostradamus's spelling of INTEL is "not quite perfect," but he maintains that it is nevertheless near enough and may in fact be a subtle joke.[2]

Michel's "discovery" is, of course, just one of many. Nostradamus is supposed to have correctly predicted a large number of events and phenomena. One of the better-known cases involves *Centuries* 9, quatrain XVI from *The Prophecies*, in which Nostradamus writes:

De castel Franco sortira l'assemblee,
L'ambassadeur non plaisant fera scisme:
Ceux de Ribiere seront en la meslee,
Et au grand goulfre desnie ont l'entree.

This may be translated into English as follows:

Out of Castile, Franco will leave the assembly,
The ambassador will not agree and cause a schism:
The followers of Rivera will be in the crowd,
And they will refuse entry to the great gulf.

The piece clearly suggests that in Spain (Castile) there will be some sort of conflict between someone called Franco and someone called Rivera. But should we treat this as a solid prediction of the fact that Francisco Franco and Jose Primo de Rivera were the two main leaders during the Spanish Civil War of the 1930s?

Let us say that we *do* treat it as such. What does this tell us about Nostradamus? Should we deem him to have been in possession of magic powers? Most residents of the UK will be able to predict with great accuracy the scene that will take place in Trafalgar Square, London, on New Year's Day, 2000. Is this also some form of magic? And are we all, therefore, prophets?

There is a difficult problem here, regarding the evaluation of predictions. If we hear it said that the prime minister of Great Britain will become a ballerina in three years' time, how should we respond? Should we treat the prediction as a wild guess, or should we deem it to have a genuine foundation? We recognize that predictions may be generated at random, and do not want to waste any attention on foundationless speculation. But to successfully discriminate the wheat from the chaff, we need to be able to decide when a prediction is to count as legitimate. And this of course brings us to the key question: What is a proper procedure for generating predictions? Or, in other words, how can prediction be *done*?

2.1 Similarity and the Nearest-Neighbor Method

In this chapter we will look at one of the most basic of all prediction (learning) methods—the *nearest-neighbor* or NN method. The method is based on the idea that prediction may be effected through exploitation of *similarity*. The guiding principle is that if we want to guess the output for a particular input drawn from a given input/output mapping, we may do so merely by looking at the outputs that are associated with similar inputs.

Using the nearest-neighbor procedure to predict missing outputs in test cases associated with a particular set of examples is simplicity itself. To guess an appropriate output for a given input, we should choose the output associated with the input's most similar case in the examples. The only prerequisite here is that all the presented input/output pairs must be stored in an accessible form. Learning in this context thus simply involves the act of *storing* the presented data.

To summarize, the nearest-neighbors learning method is a procedure of two steps.

1. Store all the examples.
2. Guess that any test case has the same output as its most similar example.

The general effectiveness of the method is readily confirmed. Imagine that we have a learning problem defined in terms of the following three examples:

```
0.6 0.2 0.3 --> 0.7
0.1 0.1 0.0 --> 0.5
0.8 0.7 0.0 --> 0.1
```

We are now presented with a single test case:

```
0.0  0.1  0.1 -->
```

What is the most likely output? Many people would guess 0.5, on the grounds that the input is a close match to the second listed input, which has 0.5 as its output. The nearest-neighbor method produces exactly the same result by the same process. The second input is identified as the closest match, and its associated output is then guessed to be the missing output.

2.2   Nearest-Neighbors in Picture Form

The nearest-neighbors method, as its name suggests, is conveniently understood in terms of geometric operations. Imagine that our examples are input/output pairs based on two numeric input variables and a symbolic output variable whose value is either x or y. For example,

```
3  1 --> y
7  4 --> x
5  6 --> x
8  8 --> y
9  4 --> y
2  5 --> x
```

We can view each input as the coordinates of a point on a plane (i.e., a 2-dimensional space), and we can represent the entire training set by drawing out the plane and labeling each input point appropriately, with either x or y. This leads to the visualization of figure 2.1 (a). In this schematic, the operation of the nearest-neighbors method simply involves guessing that a particular test case has the same output as the closest neighboring point. For example, imagine that the point labeled "?" is the test case. Operation of the NN rule involves guessing that its output is y, since this is the output associated with the nearest point.

2.3   Measuring Similarity and Distance

When we use the NN method, we have to decide how we are going to measure the closeness of a match, that is, the similarity between two data points. The most common approach involves focusing on dissimilarity or

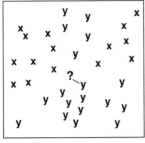
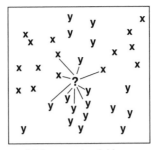

(a) First nearest neighbor   (b) 9 nearest neighbors

Figure 2.1
Visualization of the nearest-neighbors method

distance rather than similarity, since this allows us to make use of standard metric functions such as *Euclidean* distance and *Manhattan* (city-block) distance. The Manhattan distance between two items is the sum of the differences of their corresponding components. Thus, if all our variables are numeric, we can compute the Manhattan distance between two data using the formula

$$\sum_{i=1}^{n} |x_i - y_i|.$$

Here n is the number of variables, and x and y are the two data (both assumed to be sequences of numbers). The Manhattan distance function is so called because it effectively computes the distance that would be traveled to get from one data point to the other if a gridlike path is followed.

A common alternative is the Euclidean distance function. This measures the as-the-bird-flies distance. The formula for this distance is

$$\sqrt{\sum_{i=1}^{n} (x_i - y_i)^2}.$$

Deriving the Euclidean distance between two data points thus involves computing the square root of the sum of the squares of the differences between corresponding values. Figure 2.2 provides a visual illustration of the difference between the Manhattan distance and the Euclidean distance.

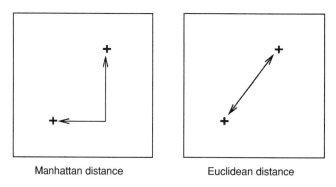

Manhattan distance   Euclidean distance

Figure 2.2
Manhattan versus Euclidean distance

Normalized Distances

In most circumstances the nearest-neighbors method produces good performance when measured against comparable methods. However, problems may arise if the data variables have very different ranges. If the first
variable varies between 0 and 1 but the second varies between −1000
and +1000, then the measurement of distances will reflect differences
within the second variable to a much greater degree than within the first.
Of course, this might be appropriate, but in general we want all our
variables to have equal status within the computation of distance. This
can be achieved by *normalizing* all difference values, for instance, by
expressing each difference value in the range 0–1. This involves dividing
the observed difference between two values by the maximum observed
difference between two values of that variable. This normalization step is
likely to be of advantage whenever data variables have different ranges.

Dealing with Nonnumeric Values

The fact that the NN method makes use of standard distance functions
whose evaluation involves finding the numeric difference between corresponding variable values means that problems arise if variables have
symbolic rather than numeric values. To get around this, some convention is required for computing the "difference" between two symbolic
values. The standard solution involves treating the difference between
two symbolic values as 1 if the values are different and 0 if they are
identical. Unfortunately, this simple solution may lead to unwanted

results if the *degree* of difference between symbolic values is significant. The only effective solution in this situation is to provide the method with some special-purpose machinery for computing the relevant values. In some cases this may involve building a difference-measuring function that embodies appropriate background knowledge.

Using More Than One Nearest Neighbor
So far we have assumed that implementation of the NN method involves looking for the single nearest neighbor. However, in practice, it is more common to look for a set of nearest neighbors of any test case and then formulate an average guess (see figure 2.1 (b)). In this case, the method is termed *k*-nearest-neighbors or *k*-NN, with the *k* representing the number of nearest neighbors used for each prediction.

If the relevant variables are numeric, the prediction is derived from the outputs of the nearest neighbors simply by numeric averaging. However, if the variables are symbolic, then the derivation may be more complex. Again, the selection of the right number of nearest neighbors to look at— the value of *k*—is something of a black art. In practice, small values in the range 2–6 are often used.

2.4   Using 1-NN to Predict the Voting Behavior of Politicians

Let us take a look at the nearest-neighbors method in action. Consider the following training set from the UCI repository of machine-learning databases.[3]

```
n y n y y y n n n y ? y y y n y --> Republican
n y n y y y n n n n n y y y n ? --> Republican
? y y ? y y y n n n n y n y y n n --> Democrat
n y y n ? y n n n n y n y n n y --> Democrat
y y y n y y n n n n y ? y y y y --> Democrat
n y y n y y n n n n n n y y y y --> Democrat
n y n y y y n n n n n ? y y y --> Democrat
n y n y y y n n n n n y y ? y --> Republican
n y n y y y n n n n n y y y n y --> Republican
y y y n n n y y y n n n n ? ? --> Democrat
n y n y y n n n n n ? ? y y n n --> Republican
```

```
n y n y y y n n n n y ? y y ? ? --> Republican
n y y n n n y y y n n n y n ? ? --> Democrat
y y y n n y y y ? y y ? n n y ? --> Democrat
n y n y y y n n n n y ? ? n ? --> Republican
n y n y y y n n n y n y y ? n ? --> Republican
y n y n n y n y ? y y y ? n n y --> Democrat
y ? y n n n y y y n n n y n y y --> Democrat
n y n y y y n n n n n ? y y n n --> Republican
y y y n n n n y y y n y n n n y y --> Democrat
```

These input/output pairs associate patterns of voting decisions with party allegiance. The input variables correspond to votes that were made in 1984. The output variable shows whether the politician who cast the votes was Republican or Democrat. Within the input, *y* indicates a vote in favor and *n* indicates a vote against. The issues upon which the votes were cast were as follows. (The numbering corresponds to the left-to-right sequence of input variables.)

1. More support for handicapped infants
2. Water project cost-sharing
3. Adoption of the budget resolution
4. Physician-fee freeze
5. El Salvador aid
6. Religious groups in schools
7. Anti-satellite test ban
8. Aid to Nicaraguan contras
9. MX missile
10. Immigration
11. Synfuels Corporation cutback
12. Education spending
13. Superfund right to sue
14. Crime
15. Duty-free exports
16. Export Administration Act, South Africa

The final case in the input/output mapping above thus records the fact that a particular Democrat politician voted *yes* to more support for handicapped infants, *yes* to the water project cost-sharing proposal, *yes* to the adoption of the budget resolution, *no* to a fee freeze for physicians, *no* to an El Salvador aid package, and so on.

Imagine that we are now presented with this test case:

```
y n n y y n y y y n n y y y n y -->
```

Applying the nearest-neighbors method (using a city-block distance and the standard convention for differencing symbolic values), we discover that the nearest neighbor of this input is number 9 (from the top) in the training set. The output value for this is Republican. Therefore, if we are using the 1-NN method, this becomes our predicted output value. The missing value is thus filled in as follows.

```
y n n y y n y y y n n y y y n y --> Republican
```

Any test case that is presented to us can be dealt with in the same way. So we can straightforwardly derive output guesses for an arbitrarily large set of test cases. In other words, we can predict the party allegiance of an individual politician merely by looking at his/her voting decisions on the relevant issues.

2.5   General Performance of 1-NN Learning

Given its extreme simplicity, the nearest-neighbors method performs remarkably well over a broad range of data. In a recent study, I was able to confirm that the method comes within an ace of the performance of C4.5, a state-of-the-art machine-learning method discussed later in the book. The study focused on 16 commonly used UCI data sets.[4] These were BC (breast cancer), CH (chess endgames), GL (glass), G2 (glass with classes 1 and 3 combined and classes 4 through 7 deleted), HD (heart disease), HE (hepatitis), HO (horse colic), HY (hypothyroid), IR (iris), LA (labor negotiations), LY (lymphography), MU (agaricus-lepiota), SE (sick-euthyroid), SO (soybean-small), VO (House votes, 1984), and V1 (VO with "physician fee freeze" deleted).

Performance figures are available for several learning methods on these problems. In particular, there is a study that gives the mean generalization rates for the C4.5 learning algorithm on all 16 data sets.[5] The figures for C4.5 were obtained by running the algorithm on 25 different training sets for each database. Each training set was created by randomly

Table 2.1
Performance comparison of C4.5 and 1-NN on common problems

Data set	BC	CH	GL	G2	HD	HE	HO	HY
C4.5	72.0	99.2	63.2	74.3	73.6	81.2	83.6	99.1
1-NN	67.31	82.82	73.6	81.6	76.24	61.94	76.9	97.76
Data set	IR	LA	LY	MU	SE	SO	VO	V1
C4.5	93.8	77.2	77.5	100.0	97.7	97.5	95.6	89.4
1-NN	94.0	94.74	77.03	100.0	93.19	100.0	92.87	87.47

selecting 2/3 of the original cases. The learning algorithm was then tested on the remaining 1/3.

In producing comparative figures for the 1-NN method, it was possible to improve on this protocol a little. The average performance of a 1-NN method on a particular data set is simply the average frequency with which the nearest-neighbor rule will give the correct classification for a randomly selected input. Thus the *expected* performance for the 1-NN method on a particular data set is identical to the average frequency with which particular inputs in the data set have nearest neighbors with the same output (classification). By computing this value for a data set, we derive the expected generalization performance for the 1-NN method. This is the value we would converge on if we performed an *infinite* number of trials with randomly selected training sets.

The figures for C4.5 and for 1-NN are tabulated in table 2.1. Note how the figures for 1-NN are generally quite close to those achieved by C4.5. In fact, the average performance of C4.5 is 85.94%, and that for 1-NN is 84.84%. The overall performance of the 1-NN method is thus just over 1% worse than that of C4.5.

2.6   Warehouse Security Example: Eliminating False Alarms

To give a flavor of possible applications of the NN method, an imaginary case study will be introduced. It will be further developed in chapters 5, 8, and 11. The case study involves a commercial warehouse.

Background
A delivery company installs a new security alarm in a warehouse containing two large rack assemblies. The alarm system works on the basis

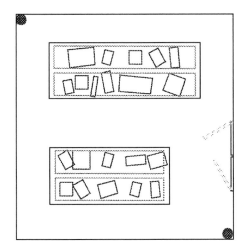

Figure 2.3
Warehouse floor plan

of signals generated by two heat sensors placed at opposite corners of the building. The general layout of the warehouse is shown in figure 2.3. The two rack assemblies are shown as long rectangles. The sensors are shown as small, filled circles in the top left and bottom right corners. The small rectangular shapes represent packages on the shelves.

The alarm system works in a straightforward way. The signals from the two heat sensors are fed to a differencing filter. This generates two output signals that correspond to the *difference* between current heat sensor signals and those generated in the previous second. The alarm is activated whenever a nonnegligible difference is obtained. Unfortunately, the system generates false alarms. These occur primarily as a result of heavy objects settling into new positions after being placed on the shelves shortly before lockup. The heat-sensing system detects the slight movement of the objects and activates the alarm even though there is no intruder within the warehouse and thus no threat of any theft taking place.

Action Taken
The delivery company decides to eliminate the false alarms by using a machine-learning approach. First, it obtains a series of example outputs

from the differencing filter. All are generated in the *absence* of any movement in the warehouse and thus represent examples of situations in which the alarm should *not* be set off. Each pair of difference values is treated as the input part of an input/output pair whose output value is 0—signifying that the input is a "negative" example corresponding to a situation in which the alarm should not be activated. A sample of the training set so produced is as follows:

```
0.004635 0.002156 --> 0
0.007348 0.001932 --> 0
0.004472 0.001955 --> 0
0.005004 0.003309 --> 0
0.00699  0.007216 --> 0
0.005207 0.006429 --> 0
```

Next the company obtains a series of outputs from the differencing filter during the settling of large objects. These also represent examples of situations in which the alarm should not be set off and thus are also turned into negative training cases.

```
0.029716 0.055003 --> 0
0.15096  0.137282 --> 0
0.057803 0.115859 --> 0
0.157733 0.188835 --> 0
0.11177  0.097654 --> 0
0.175387 0.157481 --> 0
```

Finally, the company obtains a series of outputs generated when there *is* movement of humans within the warehouse. These represent examples of situations in which the alarm *should* be activated, and are thus turned into positive training cases (i.e., given a target output of 1). A sample of the training cases generated is

```
0.390043 0.546143 --> 1
0.384668 0.601684 --> 1
0.356516 0.5978   --> 1
0.469425 0.631192 --> 1
0.49216  0.689989 --> 1
0.555335 0.498257 --> 1
0.429822 0.512558 --> 1
```

Output 1	Output 2	Alarm signal	Comment
0.00868	0.003113	-->	0	
0.051691	0.182305	-->	0	
0.053527	0.171947	-->	0	
0.086303	0.043882	-->	0	
0.112927	0.053459	-->	0	/* negligible movement discounted */
0.007048	0.007656	-->	0	
0.003551	0.007983	-->	0	
0.003427	0.006848	-->	0	
0.059901	0.108146	-->	0	
0.365832	0.458093	-->	1	/* intruder detected—alarm triggered */

Figure 2.4
Modified alarm behavior

Result

The linkage between the differencing filter and the alarm tone generator is then modified so as to enable each output from the filter to be compared (using the nearest-neighbor rule) with the given set of training cases. The alarm is triggered if and only if the nearest neighbor of the presented input turns out to be a positive example (i.e., to have an output of 1). This modification has the desired effect of discounting negligible movements and thus eliminating false alarms. The modified behavior of the alarm system is illustrated in figure 2.4. The key result here is the fifth case, in which the relatively high inputs are *prevented* from triggering a false alarm.

2.7 Notes

1. Michel was Nostradamus's first name.

2. The full text of Michel's account of Nostradamus's prediction of the Pentium scandal was made available in April 1998 as the Internet page www.alumni. caltech.edu/jamesf/pentium.html.

3. In April 1998, the UCI repository was accessible via the Internet URL http:// www.ics.uci.edu/AI/ML/Machine-Learning.html. This particular extract comes

from the 1984 United States Congressional Voting Records Database, available in the repository. The source was the *Congressional Quarterly Almanac*, vol. 40 (Washington, D.C.: Congressional Quarterly, 1985). The database was donated by Jeff Schlimmer on 27 April 1987.

4. These are the 16 data sets featured in Holte (1993).

5. Holte (1993).

3

Kepler on Mars

I don't believe in mathematics.
Albert Einstein

3.1 Science as Communal Learning

The fascination we feel with learning may have something to do with the variety and profusion with which the process occurs in the natural world. Every animal life-form does some form of learning. Certain forms of plant life also do it. And when humans do it, they do it in spades. Like any other animal life-form, humans are capable of unconscious, behavior-oriented learning. But they are also capable of carefully orchestrated, self-monitored learning activity directed toward behavioral or conceptual goals. They hone their learning skills and evaluate them using richly structured forms of measurement. They devise learning rituals and introspect on the ways in which learning may be best performed. They write books on the topic and turn individuals who show particular learning prowess into heroes.

Humans are also notable for the degree to which they engage in *cooperative* learning. Science is perhaps the grandest example of this. In science, humans use various forms of information representation—particularly language and mathematics—to transcend the individualistic constraints of learning in the animal world. The results of one learning event are preserved, shared, and passed on to future generations. Over time a resource of learning-results is accumulated. This *scientific knowledge* then serves to influence and direct subsequent learning activity.

Figure 3.1
Johannes Kepler

Although all forms of natural learning are of interest to us, cooperative scientific activity is of particular fascination due to its relative transparency. The results of the scientific learning process are explicitly represented in the form of texts and articles. And the procedures and methods that underlie the generation of scientific knowledge are often open to investigation. The history and character of scientific inquiry are thus an informative resource for any investigation of learning.

In this chapter we will look at Johannes Kepler, the seventeenth-century astronomer. Kepler (figure 3.1) is one of the most colorful heroes of science. Though born into a world dominated by religion, his fascination with the brainteaser of the time—the night sky—led him to pursue a program of increasingly mathematical research. This produced, among other things, his three laws of planetary motion. He was unusually articulate in describing his thought processes, producing voluminous notebooks describing his often erratic investigations. The things he has to say about his work are a fertile source of ideas for any study of learning. And, as we will see, they offer interesting insights for our particular approach to the topic.

3.2 Puzzling under the Night Sky

Put yourself in Kepler's shoes, taking a moonlight stroll sometime toward the end of the 16th century. The sky above you is filled with lights. Some are bright, some dim. You already know that these lights do not remain static—they move around over time. And they do not move in any simple fashion. It is as if there is a backdrop of dimmer lights moving uniformly across the sky while a small number of brighter lights move *across* the backdrop. Typically these brighter lights move more rapidly but in the same direction as the backdrop. But occasionally a light is seen to go "backwards", that is, to move in the direction opposite to the backdrop. There is a strong sense that these lights—these cosmological bodies—move in a regular fashion. The question is how to describe the regularity. How do we account for the motions of the bodies?

You have often been told that the role of the astronomer is to describe Nature, not to explain it. But you find this hard to accept. You are no heretic, though you have a weakness for mysticism. You very much want to know how the sky above your head *works*. It will never be enough simply to be in a position to predict the positions of the heavenly bodies. You have to find out *why* they come to be in a particular position at a particular time.

You are well versed in orthodox astronomy. You know that in the classical era, the Greek philosopher Aristotle formulated a model of the universe in which the planets and the sun orbited Earth (on perfect crystalline spheres) and the stars were laid out on an enclosing backcloth (see figure 3.2).[1]

You also know that a geometric formalization of the Aristotelian model—the *Ptolemaic model*—may be used to predict the positions of the cosmological bodies with reasonable success. But the Ptolemaic model is inelegant. Its predictions lack accuracy, and phenomena such as backward motion can be accounted for only by profligate addition of "epicycles." There is much to be attracted to, on the other hand, in the new *heliocentric* theory of Copernicus, which upends the Aristotelian picture by placing the sun, rather than Earth, at the center of the universe. You feel sure that there is a simple and elegant truth lurking behind complex reality. Your aim in life is to find out what that truth might be.

Figure 3.2
Medieval cosmology

3.3   Kepler's Vital Statistics

Johannes Kepler, born on 27 December 1571 in Leonberg, in what is now called Germany, was eccentric and unpopular at school. But when he attended the University of Tübingen, his intellectual abilities quickly brought him to the attention of Michael Maestlin, the astronomy professor. In private classes that Maestlin held for bright students, Kepler received his first exposure to the heliocentric theory of Copernicus. This had been published in 1543, a few days after Copernicus's death.[2]

The Copernican scheme followed Pythagoras in stating that Earth and all the other planets orbited the sun. Kepler was much taken with the heliocentric model, which appeared to offer greater simplicity and elegance than the Ptolemaic model. And later, while teaching mathematics at Graz—he narrowly avoided a career as a clergyman—he produced his own version of it.

The method by which Kepler arrived at his model was not obviously scientific. In fact his approach to scientific inquiry at this point in his career has been described in one biography[3] as "unorthodox," "crankish," "reckless," and "erratic." His duties in Graz included the preparation of astronomical calendars (horoscopes), a task at which he appears to have excelled. (A first effort successfully predicted an invasion by the Turks.) But Kepler was deeply motivated by the desire to discover the "harmonies" of the universe, and this drove him toward increasingly scientific and mathematical procedures.

3.4   The *Mysterium Cosmographicum*

In Kepler's day it was believed that there were just six planets. Kepler wanted to know why there were only six. Why not seven or five or fifteen? One day, while teaching in Graz, he came up with an idea that he felt was the greatest discovery of his life. Kepler's idea was that there are *six* planets because there are exactly *five* perfect geometric forms. These perfect geometric forms are objects that can be constructed by bringing together identical surfaces. The cube is an example since it can be constructed out of six identical squares. The pyramid is another; it can be constructed from four identical triangles. Kepler could not believe that the universe would manifest a number of perfect forms just *one less* than the number of planets by pure chance. It had to be the result of some deep, underlying regularity.

Kepler quickly arrived at a model that, he felt, put his idea on a sound footing. In this, the five perfect forms were projected out into the universe in a kind of Chinese-box arrangement (see figure 3.3).[4] Like Copernicus's theory, Kepler's model placed the sun at the center. But it departed from Copernicus in postulating that the orbits of the planets were confined to the gaps between the "shells" of the five perfect forms. The planets orbit in the way they do, Kepler argued, because of the way they are confined by the perfect solids. The solids are nested inside each other with the less complex forms on the inside, and the planets have to form their orbits in the spaces in between.

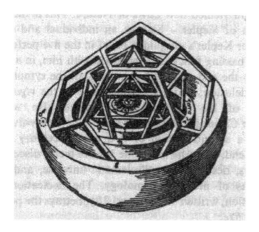

Figure 3.3
Kepler's illustration of the inner spheres

Rather remarkably, the theory worked quite well, although it was very much in keeping with Kepler's character that he dogmatically emphasized its failings. Principal among these was the fact that Kepler had to make the shells very thick to accommodate the elliptical nature of planetary orbits. However, the theory was widely regarded as appealing from the cosmological point of view, and its publication in 1596—about the time Shakespeare was writing *A Midsummer Night's Dream*—put Kepler on the map even if his theory was not treated as the fundamental breakthrough he believed it to be.

3.5   Kepler and Tycho Brahe

As a result of his success with his spheres theory, Kepler was invited to work with the nobleman Tycho Brahe (figure 3.4). Brahe was a high-flying astronomer who had amassed a storehouse of astronomical data. Derived using custom-made instruments, these data were extremely accurate for the times. Brahe had, for example, measured the length of the Earth year to within one second.

When Kepler began working with Tycho in 1600, he was instructed to focus on Mars, whose profoundly elliptical orbit was particularly difficult to explain using the Ptolemaic system. Kepler quickly realized

Figure 3.4
Tycho Brahe

that with Tycho's instruments, the motion of Mars could be observed much more accurately than it could be predicted by any existing model, including his own. Kepler immediately set about the task of creating a better predictive model of the motion of Mars.

Just one year later Tycho Brahe died. Soon after, Kepler was given the key post of Imperial Mathmaticus, an appointment that elevated his status but also brought with it a heavy burden of administrative duty. Kepler's work on Mars was seriously impeded, and he struggled on for more than eight years before finally managing to unpick the "simple regularity" of planetary motion. Although Kepler's intuition had been that planets move in circular orbits around the sun, he eventually discovered that the position of Mars could be predicted very accurately if it was assumed that planets moved instead on *elliptical* orbits.

Kepler published his discovery that planetary orbits have an elliptical shape in 1609, in a book with the title *A New Astronomy Based on Causation or A Physics of the Sky Derived from the Investigations of the*

Motions of the Star Mars Founded on Observations of the Noble Tycho Brahe. The book records the tortuous way in which Kepler approached his great insight. His almost religious resistance to the idea of elliptical orbits and his still fervent commitment to his spheres theory seem, to us, almost beyond explanation. Kepler himself notes that he really formulated the first law only when it was "forced upon him."[5]

Why should I mince my words? The truth of Nature, which I had rejected and chased away, returned by stealth through the back door, disguising itself to be accepted. That is to say, I laid [the original equation] aside, and fell back on ellipses, believing that this was a quite different hypothesis, whereas the two, as I shall prove in the next chapter, are one and the same? ... I thought and searched, until I went nearly mad, for a reason, why the planet preferred an elliptical orbit [to mine]. ... Ah what a foolish bird I have been![5]

The *New Astronomy* also contained Kepler's second law, which accounts for the way in which planets move fastest when closest to the sun and slowest when farthest away. The third law was published in *Harmonice Mundi* in 1619. Written out in sequence, Kepler's three laws of planetary motion are as follows.

1. A planet moves round the sun in an elliptical orbit that has the sun in one of its two foci.
2. An imaginary line connecting a planet and the sun sweeps out equal areas during equal time intervals.
3. The squares of the periods of planets are proportional to the cubes of the mean radii of their orbits.[6]

Kepler's laws allowed the positions of the planets to be predicted with accuracies ten times better than Ptolemaic or Copernican models. They also set the stage for Newton's discovery of universal gravitation.[7] It has to be said that Kepler did not much *like* the idea of elliptical orbits, which could not easily be accommodated within his spheres model. But his persistence as a regularity seeker drove him to accept them.

Traditionally, the role of the astronomer was simply to describe Nature. But Kepler, ever adventurous and erratic in his thinking, made the conceptually all-important leap from the descriptive mode to the explanatory mode. He wanted to explain the underlying reasons and to discover the hidden regularities. He wanted to know how Nature *worked*. His specialty was to come within an ace of a major discovery and then veer off at a wild angle at the last minute. He was fascinated by the idea that planets which are farther away from the sun move more slowly than those which are nearer. He hypothesized that there must be some kind of influence emanating from the sun which whips the planets along their paths—this was his "broomstick cosmology." But although on occasions he accurately described the concept of gravitational pull, he never used it in the attempt to explain the variations in the speeds of the planets.

In the end, the spheres model, ever at the back of Kepler's mind, made more sense to him than his three laws. And it is telling that in composing an introduction to a second edition of the *Mysterium Cosmographicum* (the book in which he originally published his spheres theory) Kepler made absolutely no reference to them. As Koestler comments:

> The three Laws are the pillars on which the edifice of modern cosmology rests: but to Kepler they were no more than bricks among other bricks for the construction of his baroque temple, designed by a moonstruck architect. He never realised their real importance.[8]

3.6 Getting It Right for the Wrong Reasons

Kepler's scientific achievement was immense. He uncovered the fundamental regularities of planetary motion and thus set the stage for Newtonian physics. He attempted to *explain* natural phenomena rather than merely observe them. In doing so he paved the way for the scientific revolution. He was one of the most successful of all scientific "learners." But his exploits seem to undermine the idea that the process of learning—individual or communal—might be carried out in any automatic fashion. If the story of Kepler tells us anything, it is that unpredictability and audacity are key.

Kepler was forever getting it right for the wrong reason. A small slip in his calculations would later lead to the discovery of a coincidence in the figures. This in turn might focus his attention on a particular aspect of the phenomenon in which he might formulate a fundamental observation. A classic example of this is to be found in his reaction to news of Galileo's discovery of previously unseen objects in the night sky.

Kepler's spheres model, recall, was based on the assumption that there were exactly *six* planets. Thus, we might expect that when, in 1610, news reached Kepler that a Paduan mathematician named Galileo had turned a telescope on the night sky and discovered several previously unidentified planets, Kepler might reasonably have felt disconcerted. But the great astronomer reacted in a quite unexpected manner. He was extremely *excited* by the possibilities opened up by the telescope, and he decided a priori that the objects Galileo had observed could not be planets since, there would then be more than six planets, in direct contradiction of his spheres theory. Kepler believed that theory to be correct. Therefore the Galilean objects could not be planets. They had to be something else.

Kepler hypothesized that they must be *moons*. And, ironically, they *were* moons. The objects that Galileo had observed were the main moons of Jupiter. Kepler's spheres theory was thus saved for the time being. However, as we now know, the solar system actually contains at least nine planets (see figure 3.5). And thanks to the growing sophistication of astronomical observation and the use of active space probes, the number of major bodies in the solar system has grown to 71.[9]

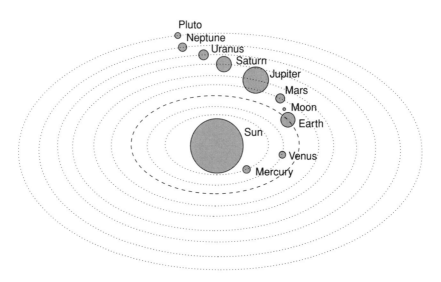

Figure 3.5
The solar system

3.7 A Footnote on Neptune

Kepler's story may carry another, more down-to-earth message for us, which is that *good luck* can make all the difference in astronomical inquiry. Consider, as an example of this, the story of the discovery of the planet Neptune. This planet, the eighth[10] from the sun, was discovered in 1846. It had been observed that the orbit of Uranus—discovered by William Herschel in 1781—deviated from the orbit predicted by Newtonian theory. The proposition was put forward that there must be some more distant planet perturbing Uranus's orbit. Efforts were then made to calculate the location of this planet on the basis of the known positions and perturbations of Uranus, Jupiter, and Saturn.

The calculations were performed independently by John Couch Adams (English) and Urbain Leverrier (French), and despite the fact that both these men had difficulty persuading others to conduct searches, the planet was eventually observed in the predicted part of the sky by Johann Gottfried Galle and Heinrich d'Arrest. Adams and Leverrier are jointly credited with the discovery of Neptune. However, there is a Kepleresque twist to the story. It turns out that the location predicted for Neptune by Adams and Leverrier contains a *large* potential error. If the search for the new planet had taken place a few years earlier or later, it would most probably *not* have been successful.[11]

3.8 Lessons from Kepler

Kepler lived an era in which there was no real separation between the arts and the sciences. It is perhaps not surprising, then, that his work was infomed as much by artistic and aesthetic considerations as it was by mathematics and logical reasoning. In retracing his steps we feel discomforted by his U-turns and wild methodological upheavals. We may feel that his work lacked rigor and scholarship. Yet we cannot help but note that the balance he struck between the two cultures enabled him to forge new paths through the space of astronomical ideas. His notebooks show that his scientific procedures were a mess. And yet, out of the mess came key insights that helped pave the way for the scientific revolution.

Kepler's work thus forms an inspiring metaphor for the "truth from trash" model that will occupy attention later on. It also raises awareness of the potential importance of the link among learning, science, and creativity. It is this aspect of Kepler that makes him a key icon for this book.

3.9   Notes

1. Internet page http://www.earthvisions.net/flat_earth.htm by Kerry Magruder suggests that the earliest manifestation of this woodcut may have been in Camille Flammarion, *L'Atmosphere: Météorologie populaire* (Paris, 1888), p. 163. Magruder also notes, "If this engraving depicts anything about medieval science, it would be the common medieval thought experiment, derived from Aristotle via Stoic commentators, regarding concepts of place and finitude: 'If you thrust your hand beyond the outermost sphere, would your hand be in a place?'"

2. The work was published with a preface by Andreas Osiander, which declared that the theory of the Polish astronomer was a "mere hypothesis" whose value lay in the way that it simplified astronomical calculations.

3. Koestler (1959), p. 242.

4. From the *Mysterium Cosmographicum*.

5. Kepler, *Astronomia Nova*, IV, cap. 58.

6. A description of the way in which the BACON method rediscovers the third law appears in chapter 8.

7. In fact, the calculations for the area law involved a numerical technique that, in hindsight, resembles integral calculus.

8. Koestler, p. 410.

9. There are in addition many thousands of asteroids and comets.

10. The extreme eccentricity of Pluto's orbit means that it sometimes actually crosses that of Neptune, causing that planet to become the ninth planet from the sun.

11. Almost unbelievably, the planet Pluto was also discovered on the basis of a predicted position that was only "accidentally" correct.

4

The Information Chicane

You promised I could say whatever I wanted.
Richard Feynman[1]

Cars run on gasoline. Trucks run on diesel fuel. Computers run on electricity. But what does learning run on? What sort of "fuel" is required to start it moving and keep it going? The question is not as bizarre as it may appear. Remember that the aim of learning can always be viewed as a prediction process. But to produce good predictions, learning obviously must make use of "properties of the world that enable predictions." Thus the fuel of learning can be thought of as these prediction-enabling properties.

But how to label them? Kepler talked about "harmonies of the universe." And terms such as "simplicity" and "regularity" and "elegance" are frequently used. Outside the academic realm, the terminology tends to be more prosaic. A novice gambler attempting to learn how to predict good horse-race winners might be instructed to focus on "form." A student doctor learning to diagnose disease might be informed that a key step is the recognition of a "pattern" of symptoms. A traffic cop trying to learn when to give chase might be encouraged to attend to "commonalities" in drunk-driving behavior. And so on.

But though there are many terms to choose from, there is really just one "substance." And the nature of this substance—*regularity*, as it will be called here—is a key issue for the rest of the book. The aim of the present chapter will be to launch the investigation by looking at some promising ideas from information theory. As we will see, this field adopts

Figure 4.1
Basic information model

an interesting angle on the issue of regularity and provides a fertile bed-rock of concepts for research on learning and cognition.

4.1   Information Theory: Starter Pack

It will come as no surprise to discover that information theory is all about information. But we need to be clear what the limitations of the theory are. Information theory shows how *amounts* of information can be measured. In particular, it tells us how much information is received by a given agent in a given situation. It is a strictly quantitative theory and does not attempt to deal with qualitative questions about what sort of "stuff" information really is. However, as we will see, the quantitative answers provided by information theory do have some interesting implications for the qualitative issues that surround it.

Information theory, as formulated by Shannon and Weaver,[2] focuses on an abstract scenario involving a *sender* agent (also known as the *source*) and a *receiver* agent. The sender is assumed to send information to the receiver in the form of *messages* (see figure 4.1). Each message is assumed to have a particular *information content*, that is, to provide a certain amount of information to the receiver. The question that information theory focuses on is How *much* information is received?

The key proposition is that the amount of information contained in a particular message must be measured in relation to the receiver's expectations. Regardless of whatever it is the message "tells" the receiver, the *amount* of information received depends on what the receiver already "knows." Imagine that the message tells the receiver it is about to rain. The receiver may already *know* that it is about to rain. In this case the message contains very little, if any, information. Conversely, the receiver may be completely unaware that it is about to rain. If so, the message contains much more information.

There is therefore an inverse relationship between level of expectation and degree of information. Information theory places this on a formal footing. It defines the amount of information of a message as inversely related to the *probability* of the message—as assigned by the receiver. Thus, a message whose content is fully expected (already known) by the receiver has a high probability and a low information content. Conversely, a message whose content is not expected has a low probability and a high information content.

The inverse relationship between information content and probability is defined mathematically as follows:

$$I(M) = -\log(P(M)).$$

Here M is the message, $I(M)$ is the information content of M, and $P(M)$ is the probability of the message (assumed by the receiver). The amount of information is thus defined to be the negative of the log of the message's assumed probability. The use of a log function here has several advantages, one being the fact that it allows information contents from different messages to be summed together.

4.2 Uncertainty

Using the basic definition of information content as a foundation stone, we can obtain characterizations for a number of other concepts. For example, we can define the amount of information that a receiver *expects* to receive from the next message—also known as the *expected information content* of a message. In doing this we follow the usual method for deriving an expected value. First we multiply the information content for each possible message by its probability of occurrence. Then we sum the products. The computed value is termed the *negentropy* of the message source:

$$negentropy = \sum_{i=1}^{n} P_i(-\log P_i).$$

Here P_i is the probability of the ith message. We can simplify the formula by moving the minus to the front of the summation. This yields

$$negentropy = -\sum_{i=1}^{n} P_i \log P_i,$$

which turns out to be identical—save for the leading minus—to the *entropy* equation from statistical thermodynamics. Hence the name "negentropy."

Moving the focus of attention away from the message source toward the receiver agent itself, we find that expected information content can be viewed as characterizing the receiver's state of "uncertainty." Here we are really just playing with words, but the step is worth taking. If the receiver expects that the next message will provide a large amount of information, then he/she/it is in a state of considerable uncertainty as to what that message will "say." Conversely, if the expected information content is low, the receiver is in a state of low uncertainty. The negentropy equation can thus be thought of as defining either the expected information content of incoming messages or the state of uncertainty of the receiver. Arguably, the latter is preferable, since it emphasizes that the computed value is related to the assumptions and internal state of the receiver, and not to any absolute property of the incoming messages.

4.3   Redundancy

The core concepts of information theory assume that a particular piece of information always translates into a *particular* message; that is, there is only one way to express a certain piece of information as a message. This is a convenient strategy since, as we have seen, it allows information content to be measured in terms of message probabilities. But it simplifies the real situation in a potentially misleading way. In reality, there will generally be many different ways to express a particular piece of information in terms of messages. And if a particular piece of information has a number of alternative renderings as a message, then it looks as if one piece of information might have many *different* information contents. If this is the case, we need to be able to decide what to focus on in determining the *true* information content.

If the information to be conveyed is clearly specified, we should be able to distinguish between parsimonious encodings of it and nonparsimonious encodings. A nonparsimonious encoding will present the information in a long-winded way, while the parsimonious encoding will provide the same information more concisely. In information-theoretic terms, we express this by saying that a particular message may contain varying degrees of *redundancy*. Any particular piece of information is assumed to have some minimum-cost, maximally parsimonious encoding. A higher-cost encoding of the same information is said to exhibit redundancy.

In the simplest situation, the information to be conveyed specifies which of some set of possibilities is the case. Let us imagine that the set of possibilities is states of the weather: *raining, sunny, cloudy,* and *misty*. A particular message must thus convey which of a set of four possibilities is the case. If, as is usual with electronic devices, communication is to be achieved by using sequences of binary digits (1's and 0's) we need to work out how many binary digits are required to construct a complete message.

Clearly, one binary digit is not enough, since this can discriminate only two states of affairs. However, two binary digits are just right, since there are exactly *four* possible combinations of two binary digits (0 0, 0 1, 1 0, and 1 1) matching up with our four possible states of the weather. Thus, in this particular situation, we know that the minimal message encoding uses exactly two binary digits per message. Anything more than this is nonoptimal and embodies a degree of redundancy.

4.4   Information in Bits

In this special case where the information to be conveyed specifies one of a set of n equiprobable states, the true information content can be computed *directly* from the number of states, since that fixes the total number of messages, which in turn fixes the probability of individual messages. If binary digits are used as the communication language, things work out particularly cleanly: the minimal message length is just the minimum number of binary digits needed to specify the n different states (i.e., it is just $\log_2 n$, where n is the number of states.)

In this situation, too, the information content of messages is very easily derived. In fact, if we use logarithms to base 2, then the number of binary digits in the minimal message turns out to be exactly the information content of the message. When we compute information content this way —using logs to base 2—the content is said to be measured in *bits*. This is a useful mnemonic reminding us that the content value specifies the number of BInary digiTS that are needed to construct a single message.

4.5   Using Redundancy to Combat Noise

Information, then, can be encoded in the form of messages either redundantly or nonredundantly. If we are concerned with the costs of communication, we will tend to favor nonredundant encodings. But in some situations, redundancy can offer advantages. For example, let us say that instead of using two binary digits to communicate the weather information, we use three bits, and always set the extra bit in each message to the relevant "parity" value; that is, we set it to 0 if the sum of the other two digits is even and to 1 if the sum is odd.

This encoding contains a small amount of redundancy. But rather than being mere wastage, this redundancy is a useful property that can be exploited to eliminate communication errors or *noise*. If a message is received whose parity bit appears to have the wrong value, then the receiver can assume that there has been an error in the communication process. The message can then be discarded or ignored. (Ideally, there will be some arrangement whereby the receiver can request a re-send.)

This process of using redundancy to eliminate noise turns out to be *universally* effective. It can be used to deal with any noise regardless of its type or degree. The general rule is that successful communication in the face of increasing noise requires an *increasing* degree of redundancy.[3]

4.6   Regularity as Useful Redundancy

The redundancy concept turns out to be particularly useful for present purposes, since it enables us to relate the subject matter of information theory back to questions about prediction and learning. To see the linkage, we need to look at the way redundancy may be exploited. When we introduce useful redundancy into an encoding scheme, we want to provide the means whereby a receiver agent can *predict* properties of parts of the message from properties of other parts. Redundancy is thus of use because of the way it supports prediction. Putting it another way, useful redundancy *is* useful because of the way it *fuels* prediction.

This takes us back to what was said at the start of the chapter. The ability to fuel prediction is the property that makes *regularity* useful. Now we see that it is also the defining property of useful redundancy.

The implication is that the substance we have informally characterized as regularity may be equated with something more technical, namely, *useful redundancy* as defined within information theory. This brings us a step closer to an understanding of regularity. But it also opens up a number of questions.

Equating regularity with useful redundancy allows us to view learning in terms of the exploitation of an informational substance. This, in turn, allows us to equate learning with redundancy elimination, which, in technical terms, is the task of *data compression*.[4] What are the implications of this? Is it the case that learning and data compression may be reduced to a common base? If so, can we press data compression algorithms into service for purposes of learning and prediction? What sort of performance might we achieve? These questions and more will be investigated later in the book (particularly in chapter 10). Initially, however, it will reward us to look more closely at the range of ways in which learning is performed in practice.

4.7 Notes

1. Comment made prior to making a speech lambasting Brazilian physics education, quoted in Feynman (1985) p. 215.

2. Shannon and Weaver (1949).

3. This is the implication of Shannon's *second theorem*.

4. Data compression is the process of reducing the size of a data set for purposes of storage or communication.

5

Fence-and-Fill Learning

In light of our review of information theory, we can characterize the actions of the nearest-neighbors method from chapter 2 in new terms. We can say, in particular, that its approach is to exploit *useful redundancy* in the form of similarity effects. But there is now a question about efficiency. We would like to know whether the nearest-neighbors method is the best way to pursue the goal of prediction facilitation through similarity exploitation. Or whether it is just one of a range of possibilities.

Remember that running the nearest-neighbors algorithm involves storing *all* the presented training data. Generation of a prediction then involves searching through the entire set of stored data for the best match to the relevant test case. For modestly sized data sets this is a reasonable proposition. But as the number of cases increases, the operation of searching for a closest match becomes expensive. If the set is infinitely large, the operation becomes effectively intractable. Clearly, then, the nearest-neighbors method cannot be regarded as an ideal method, despite its robust performance across a wide range of problems.[1]

The methodology of the nearest-neighbors method is to guess the output for a test case by looking at the case's nearest neighbor(s) among the examples. One way of visualizing what this means involves seeing the data in terms of a set of "clumps". On this view, each datapoint belongs to some clump of uniformly labeled data points, and the nearest-neighbors method operates by testing which clump a test case belongs to and producing, as a guess, the associated output label.

When we look at things this way, however, we quickly spot a promising shortcut: Why not use the clumps *directly* rather than the underlying data items? Provided that we keep track of where the clumps are located

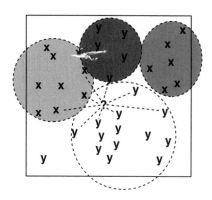

Figure 5.1
Data clumping

and how they are associated with specific outputs, we will be able to apply the nearest-neighbor rule without actually examining the original data.

Figure 5.1 illustrates this idea in a graphical form. Here we have the training set of input/output pairs from chapter 2. The main clumps in the data (i.e., the main regions of uniformly labeled data points) are circled. Once the clumps have been appropriately identified and their associated output label recorded, the label for any test case can be guessed merely by establishing which *clump* the case falls into. Using this strategy, we can throw away all the original data but still operate the NN strategy for predicting target outputs. If we use this strategy with the data depicted in figure 5.1, we get the same answer (y) as we get using the 1-NN rule.

5.1 *k*-Means Clustering

Procedures for finding and labeling clumps of data are generally termed *clustering* methods.[2] Let us take a brief look at a couple of examples. The first, *k*-means clustering, can be used to find the *k* densest ("clumpiest") locations in an arbitrary set of data points, for some prespecified value of *k*.

To run the algorithm, we work through the following four steps:

1. Randomly divide the examples into *n* sets and compute the midpoint (mean) of each set.

2. Reassign each example to the set with the nearest midpoint.

3. Recompute the midpoints of all the sets.

4. Repeat steps 2 and 3 until the assignment of examples remains unchanged.

Provided that the data naturally divide into n clusters, this algorithm eventually identifies the desired midpoints.

5.2   On-line k-Means Clustering (Competitive Learning)

The standard k-means clustering algorithm, described above, is classified as a *batch* method because it requires that all the data be presented to the algorithm in advance. However, there is an *online* variant of the process that eliminates this limitation. This takes input as it becomes available. The main steps in the method are as follows:

1. Randomly initialize n data points. Call these the *centers*.

2. Find the center that is closest to the first example and move it closer to that example.

3. Repeat step 2 using the next example, and continue until all the examples have been considered.

4. Repeat steps 2 and 3 until the examples captured by each center remain the same.

In normal circumstances, repetition of these steps ensures that the centers are "attracted" toward the cluster centers, as demonstrated by the solid black circles in figure 5.2 (a). However, problems may arise in some situations. First, we may have initialized too many centers. In this case we may have more centers than we have clusters. This will lead to some centers being "orphaned," that is, never capturing any data points at all. This is the fate of the white circle in figure 5.2(a). We may also have a situation where our random initializations of centers may mean that certain centers never capture any data points, even though there are enough clusters to go around. This problem is illustrated in figure 5.2(b).

But these problems can be safely ignored for many practical purposes. Generally, the algorithm can be relied upon to generate an appropriate clustering. Once it has been derived, each cluster may be straightforwardly associated with a unique output label. The process of predicting output labels then follows automatically. An appropriate output for any

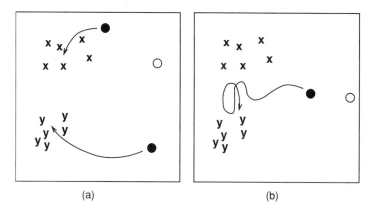

(a)

(b)

Figure 5.2
Competitive learning scenarios

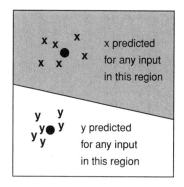

Figure 5.3
Derivation of predictions from a simple clustering

test case is generated simply by finding the input's nearest cluster and looking up its associated output. The operation is illustrated in figure 5.3.

A powerful variation on the theme of online k-means clustering is the *LVQ (linear-vector quantization)* method of Kohonen.[3] This differs from the online k-means routine in the fact that centers are attracted to captured data points at the same time that other centres are repelled. However, like standard k-means clustering, the method can be viewed as manipulating a set of nearest-neighbor decision boundaries whose number is straightforwardly related to the number of centers used.

5.3 Fence-and-Fill Learning

The clustering methods described avoid the costs of training-data storage while retaining the similarity orientation of the nearest-neighbors method. In effect, their approach is to place a boundary or "fence" around each region of uniformly labeled data points and then to "fill in" the missing data points, that is, to exhaustively populate the cluster with identically labeled data points. This effectively *eliminates* test cases and decides all possible predictions in advance. Once all clusters have been filled, every possible case corresponds to either a training data point or a filled-in data point. A suggestive name for this generic strategy—and one that will be used throughout the book—is thus *fence-and-fill* learning.

Notice how in visualizing a training set in terms of labeled data points, we effectively reconceptualize similarity as *proximity*: "similar" implies "near to" and vice versa. The exploitation of similarity is then identical to the exploitation of locality, which necessarily involves some sort of boundary-placing process.

All similarity-oriented methods thus follow the fence-and-fill theme. They attempt to locate divisions in the input space so as to pick out the relevant regions of uniformly labeled data points. Some methods aim to introduce new boundaries on a demand-driven basis; such methods may be termed *boundary-adding*. Other methods aim to manipulate a prespecified set of given boundaries; these may be called *boundary-manipulating*. Within these two broad groupings, variations are related to the type of boundary utilized and the method with which it is manipulated (or derived).

5.4 Perceptron Learning

To show how the land lies, let us review some examples of fence-and-fill learning, starting with what is often regarded as the "grandmother" of the class: the *perceptron learning algorithm* or *PLA*. Popularized by Frank Rosenblatt in the early 1960s, the PLA is based on the method of *linear discriminant function (LDF)* derivation. In its simplest form, the method involves the introduction of a *single*, linear boundary into the input space (figure 5.4). This is rotated until all the data points with one

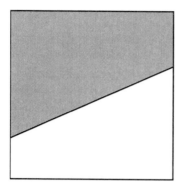

Figure 5.4
Perceptron boundary

label fall on one side of the boundary, and all data points with the other label fall on the other side.

The method by which the boundary is defined and manipulated is cunningly simple. Assuming all the input data are numeric and there is a single, binary output variable—the simplest situation—the main steps are as follows. First, a random *weight* (a random number between 0 and 1) is allocated to each pairing of an input variable with the output variable. The output for the first input is then predicted by taking the input values, multiplying them by their respective weights, and summing the results.

The predicted value is then rounded and compared against the correct output value (i.e., the value associated with the input in the training data). If the predicted value is too low (i.e., 0 instead of 1), the weights are increased a fraction. If the predicted value is too high, the weights are decreased a fraction. And since it does not make much sense to change the weight on an input variable whose current value is 0, all weight changes are made proportional to the corresponding input value. The procedure is then applied to the second training example, the third, and so on, all the way through the training set.

Provided there is some set of weights that generates correct outputs *throughout* the training set, and provided the fraction by which the weights are changed is small enough, this correction procedure—repeated long enough—is guaranteed eventually to produce perfect weights. But what is really going on here is a simple, geometric operation: the weights are the parameters of a linear boundary and the error-correction procedure is the process of trying to align the boundary so that it separates inputs with a 1 output from inputs with a 0 output. Thus, perfect weights exist only if a satisfactory linear boundary exists, and vice versa.

The perceptron learning method is easily generalized to the situation in which we have a number of output variables and our desired output values are arbitrary real numbers. The weight-update procedure is repeated for each *set* of weights associated with each distinct output variable. And the weight-change operation is changed so that the amount each weight is changed in a particular step is proportional not only to the size of the relevant input value but also to the difference between the relevant computed output value and its desired value. This yields the so-called *least-mean squares (LMS)* weight-update rule for linear regression:

$$weight_{i,j}^{t+1} = weight_{i,j}^{t} + (input_i^t \times error_j^t).$$

The rule states that the new (i.e., time $t + 1$) weight between the ith input variable and the jth output variable should be derived by adding to the current value the product of the current ith input value and the current error of the jth output variable. Provided the error of each output variable is derived by *subtracting* the computed value from the correct value, this rule always has the effect of moving weights in the right direction by an appropriate amount.

In the situation where we have a single output variable, the LMS algorithm can be summarized as a procedure of six steps:

1. Assign random values to be the initial input-to-output weights.
2. Using the first input from the training set, compute an output value by multiplying the relevant input values by the corresponding weights and rounding the result.
3. Find the error by subtracting the computed output from the desired output.
4. Modify each weight, using the derived error value and the given weight-update rule.
5. Repeat from step 2, using the next example in the training set.
6. Repeat from step 2 until the average error has been reduced to a satisfactory level.

The simplicity of the LMS procedure ensures a low computational cost. However, the restriction to one linear boundary per output variable introduces serious limitations. Within the single-output scenario, only problems involving exactly two linearly separated clumps of data points can be dealt with satisfactorily. Many problems are *not* of this form and thus cannot be dealt with by the perceptron/LMS method. Minsky and Papert[4] have demonstrated that this restriction implies an inability to learn even very simple logic functions such as two-bit parity (exclusive-or).

5.5   Backpropagation and the Multilayer Perceptron

The perceptron uses a single layer of weights to derive desired outputs. The resulting limitation is that each output value is predicted on the basis of a single linear boundary. The *multilayer perceptron* takes the idea one stage further. It uses *multiple* sets of weights (i.e., multiple linear boundaries) configured in such a way as to allow *compositions* of linear boundaries to be defined. The general result is that the method is able to deal in terms of arbitrary polygonal regions (see figure 5.5).

To understand how the MLP works, it is helpful to conceptualize the algorithm as a neural network. Instead of thinking in terms of input and output variables whose values are numbers like 0.3 and 0.74, we think in terms of *input neurons* and *output neurons* with distinct levels of *excitation*. An input variable whose value is 0.3 is then treated as a neural unit

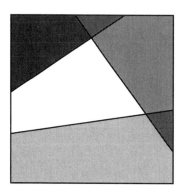

Figure 5.5
MLP/backpropagation boundaries

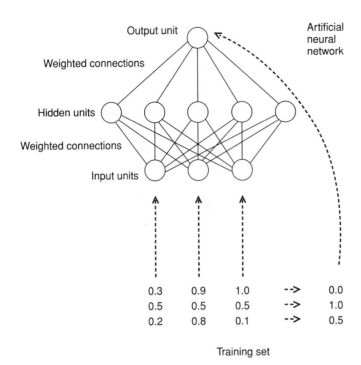

Figure 5.6
Network visualization of multiple weight sets

whose *activation level* is 0.3. The weights between input variables and output variables are treated as signifying the strength of *connections* between the relevant units. And the process of multiplying an input value by a weight is then naturally viewed in terms of the *propagation* of the input unit's activation along a connection of a certain strength.

Using this "neural network" view, we see that the perceptron's limitation is the fact that it deals only in terms of networks made up of input units and ouput units. In the multilayer perceptron, this limitation is eliminated. In addition to input units and output units, we may also have what are called *hidden units*, that is, units which have connections *from* input units (or other hidden units) and *to* output units (or other hidden units). These units play an intermediate role in the production of outputs.

To summarize, the image to have in mind with respect to the multilayer perceptron is something like the one shown in figure 5.6. This shows a neural network comprising

- A set of *input units* whose activation levels are derived directly from the input values
- A set of *output units* whose activation levels provide the computed output(s)
- A single layer of *hidden units* that are not themselves input units or output units but that have connections *from* input units (or other hidden units) and connections *to* output units (or other hidden units).

The units are represented as circles, and the solid lines represent the connections between the units. The lowermost units are the input units, the top unit is the output unit, and the units in between are the hidden units. Activation may thus be thought of as propagating upward through the network of connections. Some training data are also shown, with the arrows indicating how the input/output values are used to set the activation levels of the input and output units.

Each noninput unit in an MLP network has its own set of weights associated with its incoming connections. These effectively define a distinct linear boundary. Where we have connections from several hidden units into a single output unit, the associated weights define a *composition* of linear boundaries, that is, a region whose boundary is made up of a set of linear boundaries (the number of boundaries being identical to the number of hidden units). It is thus the upper connections that provide the ability to deal in terms of polygonal regions.

The MLP inherits the weight-update rule from the LMS procedure but adds a couple of modifications. Remember that the LMS rule is defined in terms of the error of predicted outputs. But in the MLP we have weights that do not *directly* contribute to such outputs, because they do not feed *directly* into output units. If we are to use the LMS weight-update rule, we need a way of determining the error of hidden unit activation levels.

The so-called *backpropagation rule*[5] provides a solution here. The basic idea is that although hidden units do not generate error in the usual way, they do contribute to the error of output units. By deducing the contribution made by a hidden unit to the errors of *all* the output units into which it feeds activation, we can thus derive a surrogate error value.

The method for deriving such contributions is as follows. First we obtain the error levels for all the output units by subtracting the computed value(s) from the correct value(s) in the usual way. Then we derive error values for all the hidden units that feed activation directly to output units. For each such unit, this is a two-step procedure. First, we multiply the error for each of its output units by the weight on the relevant connection; second, we multiply the sum of the results by the current activation value of the hidden unit.[6] Once the error values for the first layer of hidden units have been thus derived, error values for the units in the layer below may be obtained. The original errors are thus propagated back through the network; hence the term "error backpropagation."

Backpropagation is an important learning method that has proved to have many real-world applications. The fact that it is a generalization of the LMS regime reveals that it is essentially a similarity-oriented method. And, in fact, when it is used with limited resources (e.g., a small number of connected hidden units), it is unambiguously within the fence-and-fill class. But when the level of resources utilized increases, its membership in the class becomes more dubious. (We shall see in chapter 8 that there comes a point when it is more appropriately classified as a *supercharged* fence-and-fill method.)

5.6   Radial-Basis Functions

The *radial-basis functions (RBF)* method is a two-stage learning regime, combining a conventional clustering operation with the LMS procedure (see above), that has been shown to produce extremely good performance with certain types of data. In stage 1, the input data are processed using an ordinary clustering operation such as the *k*-means clustering algorithm. The objective in this is not the clusters themselves but their *midpoints*. Once found, these are pressed into service as the centers for radial-basis functions or RBFs. These operate in the manner of measuring devices: when given a particular input from the training set, each RBF returns a value that measures the distance (dissimilarity) of that input from the RBF's associated center. If the input is close to the center, a high value is returned. Otherwise, a low value is returned. The overall effect is that the RBFs may be used to derive a complete recoding of the training data in which each input is replaced with the responses that input evokes from the set of RBFs.

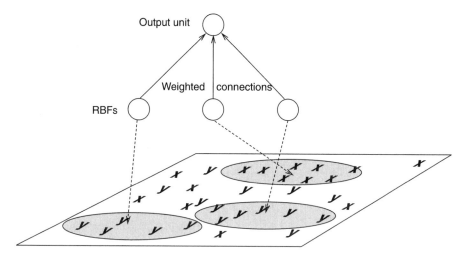

Figure 5.7
RBF network visualization

In the second stage of processing, the standard LMS procedure is applied, using the six-step procedure described above. But rather than being applied to the original training data, it is instead applied to the data recoded using the RBFs. Final outputs are then derived in the usual way. In producing predicted outputs, therefore, the RBF algorithm first recodes the input in terms of the outputs of the derived RBFs, and then processes those outputs using the derived LMS weights.

Like the MLP, RBF networks that utilize modest levels of resources (i.e., small numbers of RBFs) fall unambiguously into the fence-and-fill class. However, whereas the MLP deals in terms of compositions of linear boundaries, RBF networks may be thought of as dealing in terms of compositions of spherical (or hyperspherical) regions. As an illustration of this, consider figure 5.7. Here the two-dimensional input space is depicted lying on its side, but the training data are shown as points marked x and y in the usual way. The lower circles represent the RBF units, and the upper circle represents the output unit. Dashed lines connect individual RBFs with the clusters in terms of which they are defined. Solid lines represent the LMS connections between RBF units and the output unit.

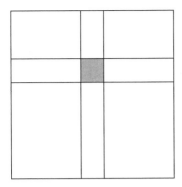

Figure 5.8
Decision-tree boundaries

5.7 ID3 and C4.5

Popularized by Ross Quinlan in the early 1980s, *ID3* is based on the idea of top-down decision-tree derivation, and thus differ markedly in style from the network-oriented methods such as MLP and RBF.[7] *C4.5*, another Quinlan contribution, enhances ID3 by adding features such as automatic decision-tree pruning. Both ID3 and C4.5 operate in an incremental fashion: they select a dimension of the input space and then place boundaries between the values of the dimension.[8] This has the effect of separating the data points into groups, such that each group associates with a particular value of the dimension (see figure 5.8). If this does not have the effect of separating the examples into perfectly uniform groups, a further dimension is selected (if available) and the process is repeated. Both methods take care to select dimensions on a best-first basis. That is, they always select the dimension in which the boundary-introduction process will achieve the best results (i.e., the most uniform subgroups).

   Like the perceptron method, ID3 is a fully paid-up member of the fence-and-fill class. Its boundary-introduction capabilities are subject to strict constraints. The dimensions it introduces cannot be placed just anywhere: they have to be aligned with one of the axes of the space (in this sense the method is actually *more* profoundly constrained than the perceptron). Moreover, the number of boundaries introduced cannot exceed the number of distinct dimension/value pairs Another limitation is that these methods, unlike LMS and MLP, only predict outputs that are explicitly represented in the training data. They do not interpolate between such outputs. This may cause difficulties if the nature of the problem suggests interpolation is required.

5.8 The Naive Bayes Classifier

Another fence-and-fill learner worthy of mention is the *naive Bayes classifier*. This derives the probability (i.e., frequency) of seeing each particular output value, conditional upon the appearance of each particular input value, within the training examples. It then uses these probability values to identify the most probable output for a given input. To understand how this works, focus on the simplest situation in which all probabilities have the maximum value of 1. (This situation occurs whenever a particular input value is *always* associated with a particular output value.) Identifying the corresponding probability effectively picks out the region of the input space in which data points have the relevant input value, and labels it with the relevant output label. Thus if all the derived probabilities have extreme values, the method works in the same manner as ID3: it generates a set of regions in which all data points share a particular input value (figure 5.8). In general, where probabilities take intermediate values, the method can be viewed as generating a probabilistic superposition of such regions.

5.9 Center Splitting

Although it is notoriously difficult to compare the performance of different algorithms, studies have tended to suggest that primitive methods such as nearest-neighbors and the naive Bayes classifier often produce excellent performance.[9] However, both of these methods have serious drawbacks in practice. The nearest-neighbors method requires storage of (and lookup within) *all* training data. The naive Bayes classifier requires computation of probability statistics with respect to *all* distinct input values, which may be extremely costly (if not infeasible) with non-symbolic data.

Beyond these methods, high performance is often associated with the decision-tree and backpropagation methods. But the former require a relatively sophisticated output-generation procedure (involving recursive descent of the decision tree), which make them unattractive to those seeking solutions with neurobiological plausibility. The latter, on the other hand, involve careful customization of user-defined parameters to obtain best performance.

What is really wanted is a method that, like C4.5, requires no parameters to be configured but, like backpropagation, permits a computationally simple output-generation procedure. To boot, the method should produce state-of-the-art performance, that is, performance at least as good as nearest-neighbors but without requiring full storage of the training data or any other impractical operation.

A promising candidate is an LVQ/C4.5 hybrid that I call *center splitting*. This adopts the center-based approach utilized in LVQ but uses the data-division operation employed by C4.5 to effectively generate new centers on the fly. The advantage is that there is no need for the user to guess in advance the number of centers that will be required.

The center-splitting method involves three main steps.

1. *Initialize.* Set the initial center to be the mean training example (i.e., the center of all the training data points).

2. *Reallocate.* Allocate to each center C the set of training examples for which C's input is nearest (using a suitable metric for the data space).

3. *Split.* Take any center C whose allocated examples have different outputs and split them into groups according to output. Delete C and, for each group, add a new center located at the mean of the group. Exit if no center has examples with different outputs. Otherwise, repeat from step 2.

After learning, outputs are predicted using the usual nearest-neighbors rule, treating the centers as the reference data points and ignoring any "degenerate" centers (i.e., centers with only one captured data point).

This method combines several attractive features in one package. We have a simple output-generation rule. We have eliminated the requirement for storage of all the training data. We also have eliminated the requirement to prespecify the number of centers. It turns out that the

Table 5.1
Performance of C4.5, 1-NN, and CS on common UCI problems

Data set	BC	CH	GL	G2	HD	HE	HO	HY
C4.5	72.0	99.2	63.2	74.3	73.6	81.2	83.6	99.1
1-NN	67.31	82.82	73.6	81.6	76.24	61.94	76.9	97.76
CS	70.6	89.9	67.19	78.87	78.77	62.62	77.73	96.1
Data set	IR	LA	LY	MU	SE	SO	VO	V1
C4.5	93.8	77.2	77.5	100.0	97.7	97.5	95.6	89.4
1-NN	94.0	94.74	77.03	100.0	93.19	100.0	92.87	87.47
CS	95.76	90.7	79.4	100.0	91.3	99.38	92.59	89.46

method also generates respectable levels of performance. On the 16 commonly used UCI problems (see chapter 2) the performance is as shown in table 5.1 (CS here denotes the center-splitting method). The figures for C4.5 and 1-NN are included for purposes of comparison. The mean performance for center splitting is 0.85, as opposed to 0.859 for C4.5. and 0.848 for 1-NN. In other words, the method's performance is on a par with an established top performer, and is actually *better* than that of 1-NN.

5.10   Boundaries of the Fence-and-Fill Class

The methods described above form a small sample of the total set of fence-and-fill methods. The *total* number of distinct fence-and-fill methods is surprisingly large and growing rapidly. Different fence-and-fill methods utilize different bounding constructs, as illustrated in the schematics review of figure 5.9. But when we describe a particular method as fence-and-fill, we are not simply stating that the method can be viewed as utilizing boundaries. *All* learning methods do this in some sense. The key property of the fence-and-fill methodology is the utilization of a limited number of *simple* bounding constructs, such as circles and rectangles and their *n*-dimensional counterparts. The emphasis on the use of simple bounding constructs reflects the underlying assumption that uniformly labeled data points will tend to exist in relatively simple regions of the input space. This, in turn, is based on the assumption that *similarity* is a key form of regularity.

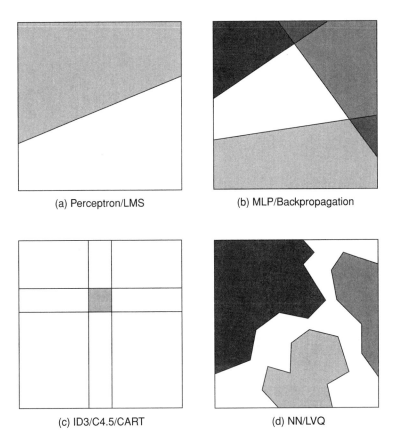

(a) Perceptron/LMS   (b) MLP/Backpropagation

(c) ID3/C4.5/CART   (d) NN/LVQ

Figure 5.9
Boundary schematics for popular fence-and-fill methods

This emphasis on similarity is the reason why such methods are often termed "similarity based" in the scientific literature. But one might equally call them "interpolative," since, when presented with a test case, they effectively interpolate the labels that are to be found around the data point's location. Interpolation is generally a deterministic operation. But in the case of learning, it is necessarily *non*deterministic, since there is no way of determining what area of input space the interpolation should be performed over; there is no way of knowing a priori how close a data point must be in order to be considered an influencing factor. Inevitably, therefore, fence-and-fill learners make assumptions in choosing where to situate boundaries.

5.11   Warehouse Security Example (Continued): 24-Hour Crisis

To conclude the chapter, we will take a second look at the warehouse security scenario introduced in chapter 2. Recall that in the initial example, the security alarm system was tending to generate false alarms as a result of being oversensitive to small amounts of movement. The nearest-neighbors method was then utilized in a process of "desensitization." The warehousing firm now decides to go hi-tech—to introduce automatic, robot stacking machines. It is hoped the change will reduce the company's payroll and also facilitate a move to 24-hour operation. Unfortunately, the actual consequence is a destabilization of the alarm system. In the original situation, the movement of *any* object within the warehouse could be treated as indicative of a break-in. In the new situation, there are robotic stacking machines moving around virtually all the time. The occurrence of movement thus no longer has an unambiguous significance with respect to security.

Figure 5.10 illustrates the new scenario. This shows (a) a robot stacking machine situated at the entrance to the warehouse and (b) the machine moving between the two shelving units. (The robot is shown as a small rectangle with an arrow pointing in its direction of motion.) To be

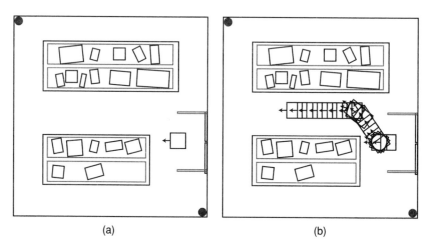

(a)   (b)

Figure 5.10
Movement of a robot stacking machine

effective under these changed conditions, the alarm system needs to discriminate types of movement exhibited by the stacking machines from the types of movement that might be exhibited by intruders.

Again, the warehousing company decides to utilize a machine-learning approach to solve the problem. A training set of positive and negative examples is obtained; they turn out to be as shown in figure 5.11. The positive examples are obtained by sampling the sensor differencing outputs in the case where there is a genuine intruder present in the warehouse, and the negative examples when there is no such intruder present. Of course, in the latter cases, the sensor difference values are often relatively high due to the motion of the robotic stacking machines. The consequence is that the positive and negative examples are not as cleanly separated as they were in the initial scenario.

The performance obtained on these data using the nearest-neighbors method with a relatively small training sample turns out to be unsatisfactory, as expected. The decision is then made to substantially increase the number of training examples and to switch to the LVQ fence-and-fill method (see section 5.2). This is applied to the data using a set of four centers, whose positions are initialized by applying several iterations of the k-means clustering operation to the input set.

The way in which the four centers are manipulated first by the k-means algorithm and then by the LVQ method is illustrated in figure 5.12. The boxes in the top row illustrate the first four cycles of k-means process-

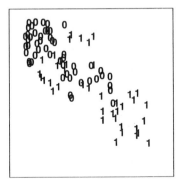

Figure 5.11
Training data for second warehouse-security scenario

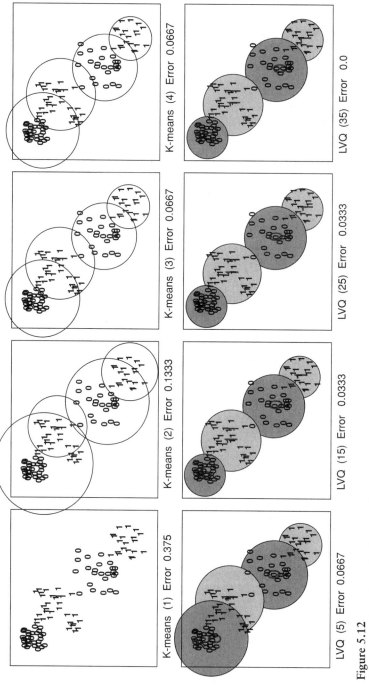

Figure 5.12
k-means and LVQ applied to warehouse-security training set

ing. The circles schematically represent the coverage of each of the four centers. As the processing continues, the examples are effectively shared out between the available centers. See in particular the enlargement in the coverage of the top row, second box. The boxes in the lower row illustrate cycles of the LVQ algorithm. In this phase, the allocations are effectively sharpened. The spheres of influence around the centers gradually come to be focused on the four main clusters of data points.

Following training with the LVQ method, the alarm system is modified so that positive outputs from the differencing filter are first classified by the LVQ algorithm for their validity. Signals classified as "negative" are discarded. Only signals classified as "positive" lead to the alarm being triggered. The achieved improvement in the reliability of the alarm system is deemed satisfactory, and life returns to normal.

5.12   Notes

1. There are ways of implementing the nearest-neighbor method that eliminate some of the search costs. However, these methods pay a significant price in terms of the increased processing complexity.

2. The investigation of clustering and numerical taxonomy methods forms a self-contained subfield of statistics. See Cole (1969).

3. Kohonen (1984).

4. Minsky and Papert (1988).

5. The backpropagation rule is generally associated with Rumelhart et al. (1986).

6. In standard backpropagation, the sum is in fact multiplied by the first derivative of the activation value.

7. The algorithm has much in common with the CART method of Breiman et al. (1984).

8. In the case where the dimensions range over numeric values, an optimal position for a single boundary is derived.

9. See Michie et al. (1994).

6

Turing and the Submarines

6.1 Moonlight Sonata

Soon after darkness on 14 November 1940, crews of the German Kampf-gruppe 100 boarded their aircraft and took off from Vannes on the Bay of Biscay. Heading due north, they crossed the Dorset coast at 6:17 and continued on their way toward the English Midlands. These aircraft—Heinkel 111s (see figure 6.2)—were the first wave of the notorious Luft-waffe raid codenamed Moonlight Sonata, a revenge attack for the RAF bombing of Munich on 8 November. The raid was to last most of the night. The target was the town of Coventry.

By early evening, incendiary devices dropped by KG 100 had started marker fires around the main target areas. Soon after, Heinkel 111s and Junkers 88s from the main force began to arrive, guided across the English countryside by the Germans' revolutionary Knickebein radio guidance system. By 10 P.M., fires were raging throughout the town—an eyewitness later described the scene as being like a "gigantic sun set."[1] By midnight the town was in havoc, although, remarkably, the cathedral tower remained standing amid the destruction, the tower clock continuing to chime on the hour while the cathedral itself blazed.

By morning, more than 1,400 people had been killed or seriously injured, and nearly three quarters of all the buildings in the town had sustained damage. None of the public utilities remained operational and a sizable proportion of the surrounding industrial installations had been put out of action.

Figure 6.1
Coventry on the morning of the November 15, 1940

Figure 6.2
Heinkel 111s similar to those used in the Coventry raid

The raid on Coventry was the first large-scale bombing raid of World War II. It provoked a massive international reaction, but like the London Blitz of the same year, it did not have the public-relations effect that the Germans appear to have expected. Despite the appalling destruction (which the British decided to play up), morale appears to have been stiffened rather than undermined. And on the industrial front, the long-term effects of the raid were not as severe as was feared. A few industrial units were completely destroyed in the raid, but the rest were all back in operation within seven weeks.

The significance of the Coventry raid for present purposes, however, has nothing to do with its scale or its military impact. Rather, it has to do with the British government's handling of secret information about the raid. In recent years, the "prior warning" story, recounted in books such as *A Man Called Intrepid* by William Stevenson, has gained currency. According to the tale, at about 3 P.M. on 14 November—the day of the raid—the Secret Intelligence Service (MI6) passed information to Prime Minister Winston Churchill regarding a Luftwaffe Enigma communication that had just been decrypted. It revealed that there was to be a major raid on Coventry that night. Supposedly, Churchill deliberated on the question of whether or not to have the town evacuated, weighing the potential loss of life against the costs of compromising intelligence operations. His final decision—so the story goes—was to do no more than alert the emergency services. According to one commentator,[2] his decision not to evacuate the town was "unquestionably the right one."[3]

Whether the town of Coventry was really sacrificed in this way in order to preserve the security of the Ultra intelligence operations remains a matter of debate.[4] But the picture is almost certainly more complex than the prior-warning story implies. There seems to be no doubt that a raid on Coventry was *expected*. But there is little evidence that Ultra intelligence figured much in the reckoning. More prosaic sources of information appear to have played a more significant role.

The town of Coventry, with its numerous industrial and munitions installations, was generally regarded as a very likely target for a major bombing raid. And expectations of a raid around 14 November were high because there would be a new moon on the following night. Over and above this, it appears that the expectation of a raid on Coventry was solidly confirmed on the *afternoon* of that day by analyses of German Knickebein radio transmissions, which showed transmission beams to be intersecting over Coventry. Whether Ultra—decrypted Enigma communications—contributed in any significant way to the buildup of intelligence about the forthcoming raid is uncertain. More than one source suggests that an Enigma communication decrypted on 14 November had specified "Korn"—a German code name for Coventry—as the target. But it is not clear whether this code word was known (at this time) to the British. Churchill, it appears, was aware that a major raid was in the offing but believed the target was to be London.[5]

The evacuation issue is also not quite so well defined as the prior-warning story would have us believe. In the weeks before 14 November, Coventry had been subjected to modest aerial bombardment on a nightly basis. As a result, many citizens of the town had fallen into the habit of traveling out to the country overnight—a practice referred to as "trekking." Those who tended to spend the night in their homes had become adept at taking cover. The net effect was that the loss of life resulting from the raid of 14 November was remarkably low, given the general level of destruction.

On the question of whether any countermeasures were put into effect against the raid, there is also considerable uncertainty. According to the prior-warning story, the only measures to be taken involved the passing of warnings to the emergency services.[6] However, there is, again, documentary evidence that standard countermeasures were put into effect by the RAF and that radio-jamming operations were also carried out in an attempt to undermine the effectiveness of the Knickebein system. (Unfortunately, due to a mathematical error, these latter efforts were applied on an inappropriate frequency and thus were rendered largely ineffective.)

The prior-warning story may thus be less than strictly accurate. But it is still worthy of consideration because of the way it mythologizes a historical phenomenon that is undoubtedly both true *and* significant, namely, the Allied exploitation of Ultra intelligence during World War II. This intelligence was derived using a technology that enabled the decryption of German communications enciphered using Enigma machines. Its successful deployment from April 1940 on meant that the Allied leaders generally had accurate knowledge of German strategic intentions. In fact, during the initial operations of the Battle of Britain, it is generally thought that Churchill was better informed regarding Luftwaffe operations than were the Luftwaffe commanders themselves.

Later in this chapter we will look at the way in which the Ultra intelligence operation was created and the uses to which it was put. But prior to that, let us briefly review some of the relevant background relating to the technology of encryption.

6.2   From Encryption to Decryption

Though the utilization of encryption is strongly associated with World War II, the technology has been employed by the military for thousands of years. Around 500 B.C., the Spartans used an encryption device called *skytale* for communicating secret military information. The encryption process involved winding some tape around a wooden baton, then writing the message *along* the baton. The tape was then unwound and sent to its destination. Decrypting the message simply involved rewinding the tape around a baton of the same dimensions and reading off the text. But without a baton of the right dimensions, nothing could be accomplished. When viewed in its unwound state, the tape appeared to contain just a jumble of arbitrary shapes.

Julius Caesar used a more formal encryption method for military communications. This involved what we now call a *substitution cipher*. (*Ciphers* are systems in which characters are replaced on a one-to-one basis. *Codes* are systems in which entire words are represented by symbols.) The encoding process involved rewriting the original message—the *plaintext*—so that each letter was replaced by a letter further along in the alphabet. The degree of shift or *offset* was varied between messages. With an offset of 2, "cat" would be encoded as "ecv," and with an offset of 3 it would be encoded as "fdw." The decryption process simply involved rewriting the encoded message—the *ciphertext*—using the inverse of the original offset.

A new twist on the substitution cipher was added by Abbot Trithemius, a Benedictine monk, in 1518. In Trithemius's method, a substitution cipher would be used to derive an initial encoding of the message.

Then, each letter in the encoding would be replaced by an associated word so as to make the encrypted message look like ordinary text. This method has the advantage of better security, but it also has certain drawbacks. The decryption process involves using information about both translations used during encryption. If the letter-to-word translations have been done in such a way as to make the encrypted text seem like ordinary text, then it may be necessary for the sender to communicate to the receiver a very large number of word-to-letter associations.

Trithemius's idea of using multiple translations within an encryption process is a powerful one, however. It can be realized in many different ways. A simple approach is to use *multiple* substitution processes, each of which employs a different offset. Decryption then has to unwind these substitutions by using the right offset at each stage. Such methods are termed *chained substitution ciphers*.

The usage of computers for communication and storage of messages opens up a whole universe of encryption possibilities. *Byte rotation*, for example, exploits the fact that each letter in a body of text is represented by the computer as a number which is itself represented in terms of eight binary digits. In byte rotation, each byte of the represented text is rotated a certain number of places.[7] The decryption process simply involves unrotating the byte the appropriate number of places.

6.3   Encryption Using Keys

One way to make a code harder to break is to *vary* the encryption process between messages. For example, if we are using a substitution cipher, we might use a different offset for each message. Under this approach, the receiver of the messages needs to know what the current variation is. The way this usually works is that the sender and the receiver agree on a *key*. This piece of information specifies which variation of the encryption process is currently being applied.[8] Each encrypted message is then decoded using a particular key.

Using keys can make an encryption method harder to crack. Even if something as simple as a substitution code is being used, using a different key with each message may prevent potential code breakers from assembling enough encrypted text in the same key to enable effective analysis to be carried out.

Unfortunately, the use of keys introduces new problems. The main difficulty is that the receiver has to know (or be told) what key the sender is using. Either the sender and receiver have to agree in advance what keys will be used for all future messages, or the sender has to have some way of communicating the current key to the receiver. Both situations introduce new security risks.

An example of the former approach is the *onetime pad*. This is like a notebook, each page of which specifies a different key. Each time the sender sends a message, the key specified by the top page in the notebook is used. The page (and key) is then discarded. The receiver, who has an identical copy of the onetime pad, uses and then discards the keys in the same sequence as the sender. Thus all messages are decrypted correctly. But a code breaker looking at the encrypted data sees what is, in effect, an ever-changing encryption process.

6.4   Decryption Issues

In some situations, code breaking (*cryptanalysis*) can be quite straight-forward. Let's say we suspect a simple substitution code is being used in a particular context. To break the code, we simply need to discover the offset. One possibility is to carry out a statistical analysis of the encrypted text. This may unearth the fact that the character which appears most frequently in the encrypted data is "j." Since "e" is the character that appears most frequently in ordinary English text, we may guess that "e" is encoded as "j" and that the offset being used is thus 5. To find out if this is correct, we see what happens when we translate the text using an offset of −5. If the output generated is meaningful text, we have broken the code.

Substitution ciphers are among the simplest and easiest to break of all encryption methods. Modern encryption methods tend to be much more secure. And they typically depend for their security on the use of keys. Effective code breaking, then, usually involves an exhaustive search through a space of known keys. In this approach, the code breaker knows how to carry out the translation with respect to a specific key but needs some way of checking the validity of each possible key. The way this is done varies, depending on the resources that are available to the code breaker. Possible resources include

• Known plaintext: the correct translation for a given sequence of ciphertext
• Chosen plaintext: the correct translation for any sequence of ciphertext
• Chosen ciphertext: the correct encoding for any sequence of plaintext
• Adaptive chosen plaintext: correct translation/encoding for any sequence of ciphertext/plaintext.

For modern encryption algorithms, exhaustive search of all possible keys is often the *only* effective method of decryption. In this context, the power of the encryption method is determined by the length of the key, since this determines how many possible combinations there are. Longer keys yield more secure codes. Extremely long keys should thus yield codes that are *extremely* secure. However, caution is advisable. Using a network of 100 computers, a student recently managed to break a message coded with a 40-bit key in just eight days. Thus 40-bit keys would appear to be not long enough. In fact, commonly used encryption systems tend to have a key length of 128 binary digits or more. A 128-bit key length would present a decipherer trying to attack such a code by brute force with a search through approximately 1,000,000,000,000,000,000,000,000,000,000,000,000,000 (one million million million million million million) possible variations.

6.5   Public-Key Encryption and the RSA Method

Use of private keys (also known as *secret keys*) introduces a catch-22 into the encryption process. To achieve flexibility, the sender has to be able to communicate the key used to the receiver. But this creates a new security problem: How to communicate the key without potential code-breakers getting hold of it?

The solution to this problem came from American cryptographer Whitfield Diffie. His invention, in the mid-1970s, of *public-key encryp-*

tion triggered a revolution in cryptology. The essence of the idea is relatively simple. In a public-key system, every receiver has one *public key* and one *private key*. The receiver makes the public key publicly available but keeps the private key secret. Anyone who wants to send an encoded message to the receiver encodes the message using the public key. But the message can be *decoded* only by using the private key. Thus, in this system, anyone can send a safely encrypted message to anyone else, provided the relevant public key is known.

A leading public-key method is *RSA encryption*. This is a public-key cryptosystem for both encryption and authentication, invented in 1977 by Ron Rivest, Adi Shamir, and Leonard Adleman. The security of the RSA method relies on the mathematical process of prime factorization. This is believed to be an *inherently* complex task, requiring huge amounts of computation in general. However, no proof of this assumption exists. Thus there is always the possibility that RSA encryption might turn out to be much less secure than assumed.

The main threats to the safety of public-key systems are developments in computing power and in mathematical theory. The former threat is, however, of less concern than might be imagined. Even assuming that the power of computers will continue to increase at the rate of the last two decades, cryptographers assume that messages encrypted with current technology will be safe for around 100 years. The mathematical threat, however, is more pressing. And it is interesting to note that in 1993, RSA Data Security, vendors of the RSA method, set up an ongoing prime-factorization competition. The original announcement of the competition begins as follows.

RSA Data Security hereby announces that it is sponsoring an ongoing "factoring challenge" (with cash prizes) to encourage research in computational number theory and the pragmatics of factoring large integers. RSA Data Security specializes in cryptographic products, particularly those based on the RSA public-key cryptosystem. The results of this challenge will help users of the RSA public-key cryptosystem achieve the level of security they desire.

RSA Data Security's aim in setting up this competition is, of course, to attempt to keep tabs on cutting-edge mathematical work that might have an impact on the task of prime factorization and thus undermine the security of the RSA coding system.

Figure 6.3
Enigma encryption machine (army version)

6.6 The Origins of Enigma

Within the general landscape of encryption technologies, the Enigma
encryption system, utilized by German forces during World War II, represents an important landmark. The Enigma system actually predated the
invention of public-key systems. However, it did utilize a key-passing
methodology. The Enigma cipher was essentially a complex substitution
cipher using typewriter-like machines (see figure 6.3) that, thanks to a
network of interconnected rotors, were able to apply a continuously
changing substitution mapping.

Each Enigma machine had a number of manually adjustable parts that
affected the way in which a message was encrypted, the settings of these
components forming the "key" for a given message. During World War
II, Enigma machine settings were adjusted on a regular basis, sometimes

as often as every eight hours. In addition, each Enigma message incorporated its own individual key, and this was, in later operations, randomly selected. In order to decrypt an Enigma message, it was therefore essential to know the construction of the machine, the initial settings and movements of the adjustable parts, and the identity and meaning of the incorporated key.

It is generally believed that Enigma codes could have been effectively unbreakable if the full potential of the machines had been utilized from the earliest days. However, the Germans began to tighten procedures only when it was already too late. Enigma traffic was initially broken by Polish cryptographers in the early 1930s, an achievement that was based on firsthand experience of parts of a working Enigma machine and mathematical analysis of wiring permutations. The Poles maintained an ability to decode Enigma communications until 1938, when the Germans improved operator procedures in a number of ways—in particular by having operators set their machine configuration at random.

The Poles lacked the resources to combat this new regime. And with the deteriorating political situation they decided, in July 1938, to hand their work over to the British and French. This intelligence gift included two Enigma machines (manufactured in Poland) and, according to some sources, an early "bombe" machine. The latter utilized several interconnected Enigma machines for decryption purposes and was the forerunner of the machines used by the British and Americans during the war.

It is at this stage in the story that Alan Turing (figure 6.4) comes on the scene. Turing, born on 23 June 1912, obtained a distinguished degree in 1934 from King's College, Cambridge. In the following year he became a fellow of the same college, and in 1936 received the Smith's Prize for his work on probability theory. In these early years, Turing seemed destined to follow a conventional, academic path. His far-reaching interests and special talents, however, soon took him in a quite different direction.[9]

Turing's work in the mid-1930s led to the publication of a paper on the question of decidability, or the *Entscheidungsproblem*: the question of whether there could exist, in principle, a method by which all mathematical questions could be decided. In showing that no such method can exist,[10] Turing made use of the concept of an imaginary computational

Figure 6.4
Alan Turing

machine—the so-called *Turing machine*—and this led him to a deeper interest in computation. His investigations encouraged him in his belief that a computational machine could in principle engage in rational thought in much the same way as a human being.[11]

After spending two years as a graduate student at Princeton University, Turing returned to Cambridge in 1939. He was then recruited to work part-time for the British cryptanalytic department, the Government Code and Cypher School. This led directly to his wartime work at *Bletchley Park*, the secret British code-breaking center that played a key role during World War II.

6.7 Building Bombes

Building on the work done by the Poles, Turing and his colleges at Bletchley were able to build sophisticated decryption machines ("bombes"). Using these, they were able, by early 1940, to crack the simpler form of Enigma code used by the Luftwaffe. As a result, Churchill and the RAF command had reliable information about German strategy from the earliest days of the Battle of Britain. This they used to great advantage, employing a kind of guerrilla warfare against the numerically superior Luftwaffe forces.

The more complex form of the Enigma code used for U-boat communications, known to Bletchley Park as Dolphin, was first cracked in early 1941, although it could not be read without delay until the summer of that year. The result was that throughout most of 1941, the Allies were able to track U-boat positions and strategic intentions. Shipping losses in the North Atlantic were dramatically reduced. However, in Febuary 1942, possibly aware that their communications were being read by the British, the Germans increased the sophistication of their Atlantic and Mediterranean Enigma system, creating a new cipher and adding an extra rotor to the encryption machine. As a result, the complexity of the signal-breaking task increased massively. Decryption operations at Bletchley Park were brought to a grinding halt, at least with respect to naval communications.

Working flat out throughout 1942, Turing and his colleagues fought to restore the ability to decrypt naval signals. The task entailed the development of more sophisticated mathematical techniques, and their consolidation in still more complex versions of the bombe machine. The Bletchley Park team was helped in these efforts by the fact that, at one setting, the new Enigma machine (M4) emulated the old machine (M3). They were also able to make use of a codebook captured from a U-boat at the end of October. However, the task they were confronted with was still monumental, and decryption ability was not fully restored until mid-December. Throughout most of 1942, therefore, the Allies were effectively blind to naval communications. They had no easy way of tracking U-boat positions and were thus unable to predict where an attack might be made. The consequences for convoys in the Atlantic was inevitably disastrous.

With the restoration of decryption capability at the end of 1942, the situation began to improve. And from early 1943 on, the Allies were able to read naval signals on a more or less continuous basis for the duration of the war, despite the fact that the Germans tightened their coding arrangements from time to time. As a result, many thousands of tons of shipping and countless lives were saved. But the general tactical advantage provided by the continuous supply of Ultra intelligence is only now beginning to be fully evaluated. Churchill himself described Bletchley Park as "the goose that laid the golden egg and never cackled." Other wartime leaders have noted the key role that Ultra played in the achievement of victory

Turing's role within Ultra is now widely recognized as having been of crucial importance. He was a key figure in the development of the first British bombe machine and, in early 1940, was involved in liason with the Polish mathematicians.[12] However, his character was not at all that of the traditional national hero. In fact, his working practices at Bletchley Park were regarded as somewhat eccentric. Hodges notes:

Alan Turing was the genius loci at Bletchley Park, famous as "Prof," shabby, nail-bitten, tie-less, sometimes halting in speech and awkward of manner, the source of many hilarious anecdotes about bicycles, gas masks, and the Home Guard; the foe of charlatans and status-seekers, relentless in long shift work with his colleagues, mostly of student age.[13]

Turing's work on decryption and computation—his MOSAIC design of 1945 may have been the first complete description of a general-purpose computer—is only now beginning to be fully appreciated. At the end of World War II, he went to work at Manchester University, where he continued his pathbreaking work on computation. However, in March 1952 he was arrested and charged with having a homosexual relationship. In court, Turing chose to accept a one-year course of estrogen injections instead of a prison sentence. He died just two years later, in mysterious circumstances. The coroner declared him to have committed suicide.

6.8   Encryption and Learning

The story of the Enigma work in World War II is intriguing. And as long as some of the documentary evidence remains classified or otherwise unavailable, it will continue to generate heated debate. For present purposes, the story has a special significance because it concerns what is, in effect, the first attempt to apply a form of *machine learning* to a serious

practical problem. That the process of automatic decryption is a variation on the theme of learning is readily shown. Both processes involve the
attempt to exploit regularities in raw data. And both take prediction of
unseen data to be a criterion of success. The differences between the
processes have largely to do with the context in which they operate and
the character of the problem presentation.

The relationship between learning and decryption is perhaps best
illustrated using an example.[14] Consider the following ciphertext.

```
HCALN UQKRQ AXPWT WUQTZ KFXZO MJFOY RHYZW VBXYS IWMMV WBLEB
DMWUW BTVHM RFLKS DCCEX IYPAH RMPZI OVBBR VLNHZ UPOSY EIPWJ
TUGYO SLAOX RHKVC HQOSV DTRBP DJEUK SBBXH TYGVH GFICA CVGUV
OQFAQ WBKXZ JSQJF ZPEVJ RO -
```

This is the first section of a three-part Enigma message sent to German
Army Group Command #2 on 21 September 1938. Decoded into German, this part of the message reads:

```
AUF BEFEHL DES OBERSTEN BEFEHLSHABERS SIND IM FALLE X Z X ZT X
UNWAHRSCHEINLICHEN X FRANZOESISQEN ANGRIFFS DIE
WESTBEFESTIGUNGEN JEDER ZAHLENMAESSIGEN UEBERLEGENHEIT ZUM
TROTZ ZU HALTEN X.
```

(The plaintext contains fewer characters than the ciphertext due to
the fact that the initial six characters in the ciphertext are the key, and the
third group of five characters is an identifier.) When we translate the
German for the three parts of the complete message into English, we
obtain the following text.

```
The Commander-in-Chief orders as follows:


In the case of French attacks on the western fortifications,
although unlikely at this moment, those fortifications must be
held at all costs, even against numerically superior forces.


Commanders and troops must be imbued with the honor of this
duty. In accordance with orders, I emphasize that I alone have
the right to authorize the fortifications to be abandoned in
whole or part.
```

I reserve the right to make changes to order OKH/Gen/St/D/H 1.
Abt. Nr. 3321/38 GKDos of July 1938.

The Commander-in-Chief of the Army

In the context of an encrypted communication such as this, the decryption task involves mapping the ciphertext onto its corresponding plaintext translation. Generally, "cribs" are available that show how certain sequences of ciphertext translate into plaintext. Thus we can imagine that the code breaker is effectively presented with a mapping between sequences of ciphertext and sequences of plaintext in which only some of the plaintext sequences are given. Using the first part of the army message given above, the mapping might be constructed as follows.[15]

```
Q K R Q W U Q T Z K --> A U F B E F E H L D

F X Z O M J F O Y R --> E S O B E R S T E N

H Y Z W V B X Y S I --> B E F E H L S H A B

W M M V W B L E B D --> E R S S I N D I M F

M W U W B T V H M R --> A L L E X Z X Z T X

F L K S D C C E X I --> U N W A H R S C H E

Y P A H R M P Z I O --> I N L I C H E N X F

V B B R V L N H Z U --> R A N Z O E S I S Q

P O S Y E I P W J T --> E N A N G R I F F S

U G Y O S L A O X R --> D I E W E S T B E F

H K V C H Q O S V D --> E S T I G U N G E N

T R B P D J E U K S --> J E D E R Z A H L E

B B X H T Y G V H G -->

F I C A C V G U V O -->

Q F A Q W B K X Z J -->

S Q J F Z P E V J R -->
```

The goal, then, is to derive the means of predicting the missing portions of plaintext (a task that is *particularly* hard, since these pairs do not include the key information of the plaintext encoding of message length etc.). But this simply brings us back to the standard prediction scenario involving a mapping in which some of the output elements are missing. The decryption task thus turns out to be straightforwardly mappable onto the learning task. The two tasks are variations on the same fundamental theme.

What this tells us is that the Bletchley Park operation and the Polish work that preceded it constitute the first and perhaps most dramatic example of large-scale computational learning. But there is something more. While the problem posed by the Enigma system is clearly a kind of "learning" problem, it is nevertheless quite different from the type of problem that we have looked at in previous chapters. It cannot be solved simply by mapping out the statistical correlations that are manifest in the data, as might be done by the k-NN method, for example. Rather, it involves identifying and disentangling the *relationships* that exist in the data, utilizing available knowledge about the processes that generated those effects.

This form of learning—*relational learning*, as it will be called from here on—represents a new departure in the study of automatic learning procedures. The implementation of the process is a significant challenge from the engineering point of view. But a better understanding of what relational learning involves paves the way for connections with other forms of mental process and particularly with creativity. The investigation of relational learning as a computational procedure will be the concern of the next chapter. The investigation of the connections that the process has with creativity and related processes will be a primary concern for the rest of the book.

6.9 Notes

1. Longmate (1976).

2. Winterbotham (1974).

3. This same commentator goes on to note, "I am glad it was not I who had to take it."

4. However, it is known that Churchill was prepared to allow naval convoys to come under attack from U-boats rather than compromise Ultra security.

5. This is reported by Colville (1985).

6. An event that is itself disputed. See Longmate (1976).

7. To rotate a byte by one position, we simply put the last binary digit into the first position and move all the other digits along one place. To rotate the byte several positions, we simply repeat this operation several times.

8. The term "key" has two meaningful connotations here. We can think of it as the thing that is used to "lock" the message. We can also think of it as being something like a musical key, a particular variation in which the encoding process is carried out.

9. Hodges (1992).

10. Turing's demonstration was made roughly simultaneously with that of the American logician Alonzo Church.

11. Turing's article "Computing Machinery and Intelligence" (1950) is one of the seminal papers in the field of artificial intelligence.

12. The degree to which the British failed to involve the Enigma-experienced Polish cryptographers in the Bletchley Park operation is a matter of controversy.

13. Hodges, A. *Alan Turing—A Short Biography*. Part 4. Currently available at www.turing.org.uk/turing/lio/part4.ntml. For a printed version, see Hodges (1992).

14. This is based on the example analyzed by Frode Weierud at

http://www.gl.umbc.edu/lmazia1/Enigma/enigma.html

and by Bill Momsen at

http://www.gl.umbc.edu/lmazia1/Enigma/enigma.html.

15. In constructing these pairs I have taken each part of the original message and deleted both the initial string specifying the key and the dropped-in identifier, so as to obtain a 1-to-1 mapping between characters in the ciphertext and the plaintext. I have then split the message parts into conveniently lengthed sequences and arranged them into an input/output mapping.

7

The Relational Gulf

7.1   A Meeting at the Crown

In the public bar of the Crown Inn at Shenley Brook End (figure 7.1), an imaginary meeting takes place between Alan Turing and Johannes Kepler.

Turing: Long time, no see.

Kepler: Yes. Unfortunately, I don't get about as much as I used to. But when I received your message, I came at once.

Turing: It was most kind of you.

Kepler: Nonsense! This Enigma problem of yours sounds intriguing. And I need something to take my mind off Mars. It's driving me mad.

Turing: But you have good data.

Kepler: Certainly, we have good data. Excellent-quality data. Brahe's instruments are second to none. But data alone cannot tell you much.

Turing: Ah, you're so right. Back at Bletchley my desk is covered with teleprints. The radio boys are intercepting hundreds of signals a day now. It's an avalanche.

Kepler: But you have these machines, yes? You put the numbers in the milling machine and out come results.

Turing: It's not so easy. You have to wire up the milling machine so that it does exactly the right thing. It's a huge task.

Kepler: Of course, there is always a catch. I recently had an audience with ... you know who. Can you imagine what he said?

Turing: What?

Kepler: He said Brahe will go down in history as the man who captured the motions of the planets. Or words to that effect. I nearly choked. I

Figure 7.1
The Crown Inn

tried to explain in words of one syllable that Brahe had given us very accurate data. But that he had *not* provided us with the means of interpreting those data.

Turing: So few people understand the importance of prediction.

Kepler: It makes it impossible to get any work done. There are so many distractions. My mother has been accused of witchcraft again. Did you know?

Turing: I'm sorry.

Kepler: Yes. I think she can dodge it, though. But what with my administrative duties and my family problems, I am making no progress at all. I just go around in circles. I look at the Mars figures and they make no sense. That planet simply does not behave itself properly. It's affecting my health.

Turing: You shouldn't despair. I felt the same way last year. It's only natural. Staring at something incomprehensible and doing it for hours and days and sometimes weeks on end can be a terrible strain. On the other hand, you have to be alert all the time. I don't know about you, but I see letters and figures everywhere. I can't help trying to read some sort of meaning into them. Car numbers. Telephone numbers. If they begin with 66 and end with 44, I start thinking that must have some significance. It's ridiculous.

Kepler: But now you have made a breakthrough?

Turing: We seem to have cracked the simpler code, yes.

Kepler: How wonderful that must be.

Turing: You should come and work with us. No one tries to devalue what we're doing. Quite the opposite. Churchill thinks we're magicians, evidently.

Kepler: Maybe he's right?

Turing: No, there's no magic. The Poles had paved the way. *Brilliant* mathematicians, some of them. Fortunately, they started working on Enigma when the Germans were still being very slack. The Nazi operators evidently can't resist the temptation to use the names of female parts for their keys. [laughter] All we've done is pull together the scraps of information. And of course we've made the Bombe ... the milling machine bigger and faster. But the basic ideas are really quite simple. Once you start thinking about it, there are lots of ways to eliminate possibilities. When you begin putting it all together, you find that the numbers are getting very reasonable. Then it's just a question of making the machine go as fast as possible.

Kepler: I wonder if I could use your milling machine on the Mars data.

Turing: Well, not this particular machine, probably. But I have some ideas for a machine that might be of use to you.

Kepler: Ah, yes. Your paper-tape machine. But it's just an idea, yes?

Turing: For now.

Kepler: But even with a machine, you still have to tell it what to look for.

Turing: Yes, this is true.

Kepler: And that is what concerns me, you see. I cannot quite decide what it is that I'm looking for.

Turing: The truth?

Kepler: That's a bit vague, don't you think? We two, we're just the same. We look at our data and we try to find something in the data that enables us to reconstruct. To explain.

Turing: To predict?

Kepler: Yes, to predict. But what is this thing we are looking for?

Turing: Factor X?

Kepler: What is this factor X? What is the nature of the substance?

Turing: We look for patterns.

Kepler: But then one needs to ask, What is a pattern?

Turing: OK. We need to make it more general. Could we say that we are searching for simplicity?

Kepler: Yes, that is better. We look for simplicity within complexity. But to me it is also a kind of harmony. Or maybe even, may I say it, a kind of beauty.

Turing: I don't know. Some of the Enigma procedures are a terrible mess.

Kepler: And anyway, what's the good of talking about harmony and beauty? These are things we could never explain to your machine.

Turing: I'm not so sure. When I've had the thing built, we can try it out.

Kepler: I'll look forward to that.

Turing: Let's drink to it, then. Here's to beauty!

Kepler: Harmony!

Turing: Simplicity!

Kepler: Elegance!

Turing: Pattern!

Kepler: Form!

Turing: Lawfulness!

Kepler: Predictability!

Turing: And not forgetting, *of course*, the destruction of the Nazi war machine!

Kepler: Well ...

Turing: What's the matter?

Kepler: I'm not sure I can go along with that. After all, I am, in some sense, a German.

7.2   Factor X: The Real Enigma

We cannot be sure that this is how Kepler and Turing would have communicated. In fact, we cannot be sure that they would have been able to communicate at all. But if they had been able to converse, they would probably have found they had much in common. They surely would have recognized that Kepler's attack on the Mars data and Turing's attack on the Enigma data were both part of the same battle—the battle to identify, within raw data, properties enabling the prediction and interpretation of those data. And, in attempting to pick Turing's brains regarding the *nature* of the mysterious prediction-enabling properties, the imaginary Kepler is effectively articulating the key question of this book. When we attempt to use a body of data to discover a way of predicting those data, we hope to exploit certain properties. But what *are* these Enigmatic properties?

We have seen that there is no shortage of suggestive terminology. Prediction-enabling properties of data may be referred to as patterns, trends, regularities, harmonies, and so on. But switching from one term to another does not get us very far. Slightly more usefully, we have seen (in chapter 4) that regularity may be equated with useful redundancy, as defined by information theory. But although this gives us a mathematical understanding of the *effect* that the exploitation of regularity should have, it does not give us what we really want: a characterization of what regularity *is*. With respect to this question, we are still largely in the dark. As a cryptographer might put it, we are blind.

The aim of the present chapter, then, is to obtain better illumination on this central issue. But our approach to the problem will not take the form of a Coventry-esque, full-frontal assault. Rather, it will be made in the style of the Bletchley Park code breakers. We will come at the problem obliquely. The aim will be to throw some light on the question by gathering together innocent-seeming scraps of information—to clarify the nature of prediction enablement through a process of problem division and case elimination.

7.3 The Explicitness Distinction

Certain facts about regularity are uncontroversial. Regularities that appear within certain data are properties *of* those data, and as such may be classified as explicit or implicit. Prediction thus must exploit explicit or implicit properties. In the former case, where the prediction is based on the exploitation of explicit features of the given data, the predicted data must obviously be made up of elements that are explicitly within the original data. Such predictions must, therefore, exploit explicit *commonalities*.

In an implicit regularity, on the other hand, the explicit elements of data are insignificant by definition. (If this were not the case, the regularity would classify as *explicit*.) The implication is clear: the significance must attach to a mutual property of the elements, that is, it has to be the relationship between the elements which is significant.

Logically speaking, then, prediction has to work in one of two quite different ways. Depending on the character of the regularity being utilized, it may exploit (explicit) commonalities or (implicit) relationships.[1] An alternative and arguably better way of drawing the explicit/implicit distinction is thus to say that regularities may appear in either a *relational* or a *nonrelational* form, since in one case we have the exploitation of relational regularities, while in the other we have the exploitation of nonrelational regularities.

Following this argument to its logical conclusion, we identify two distinct styles of *learning*:

• Relational learning: learning oriented toward exploitation of relational regularity
• Nonrelational learning: learning oriented toward the exploitation of nonrelational regularity.

The implicit/explicit distinction thus expands into a generic, two-way classification scheme that allows us to distinguish between relational and nonrelational forms of both regularity and learning. But what makes the scheme of more than mere academic interest is the fact that the expected complexity of the two forms of learning looks to be *very* different. The number of possible nonrelational regularities in a given data set is just the number of possible *combinations* of explicitly represented elements. If the data set is finite, then so is the number of possible combinations. The number of possible nonrelational regularities in a given case is thus generally *finite*. Relational regularities, on the other hand, are identified in terms of relationships between data items. The number of potential relationships in a given scenario is generally unbounded, implying that the number of possible relational regularities is *infinite*.

Nonrelational learning, then, looks to be a procedure of *finite* complexity, while relational learning looks to be a procedure of *infinite* complexity. This is about as far apart as two operations can be in terms of complexity. Learning thus appears to be more straightforward on the nonrelational side. To put it crudely, relational learning looks to be the "tough nut" and nonrelational learning the "soft option."

7.4 NonRelational Learning Is Similarity-Based Learning

Consideration of the difference between explicit and implicit regularity leads us to classify learning processes under two headings: relational and nonrelational. But are these categories merely theoretical constructs? Or do they have genuine cash value? And how should the practical learning methods we have looked at so far—LVQ, backpropagation, ID3, and so on—be classified?

On the relational side, things *seem* to click into place rather easily. There is a well-defined subfield of machine learning that concerns itself with a process termed "relational learning," which does indeed seem to encompass methods that aim to exploit properties identified in terms of relationships.[2] Thus, the theoretical category of relational learning looks to have a readily discerned instantiation in the real world of machine-learning research.

Unfortunately, there is no complementary subfield for the nonrelational category. No paradigm exists within machine learning (or any related enterprise) that explicitly concerns itself with the process of "nonrelational learning." And although the mutual exclusivity of the relational/nonrelational categories seems to imply that any learning process not characteristically relational must be characteristically *non*relational, there is something unsatisfactory about identifying the nonrelational category with the part of machine learning that is "left over" when we exclude the overtly relational part. Something more principled is required.

7.5 Incidental Effects

Let us rewind the story a few frames. Recall that the goal of a learning process may be conceptualized as a form of prediction. This process, we have seen, necessarily involves the observation of a "connection" between certain observed elements of data that, by extension, implies the existence of certain unobserved elements of data. In the relational case, the connection is simply a particular relationship. In the nonrelational case it is, as we saw above, the sharing of common elements, or syntactic similarity. Nonrelational learning therefore involves the exploitation of syntactic similarity effects, exactly the "similarity-oriented" process that was examined in chapters 2 and 5. And insofar as this *is* the bit of machine learning left over when we remove the overtly relational part, we have the expected result. The theoretical situation thus seems to be neat and tidy, with methods and problems tucked away in two quite distinct complexity classes. But, unfortunately, the practical classification of methods and tasks turns out to be a much harder trick to perform.

Let us focus on task classification. At first sight, it looks as if it should be possible to classify supervised-learning tasks (i.e., tasks based on an input/output mapping) as relational or nonrelational, depending solely on the degree to which the data show signs of being tractable to similarity-based methods, that is, the degree to which the data exhibit similarity effects. But it is not obvious how to operationalize this idea.

Imagine that the data available to the learner agent take the form of combinations of values of variables—the most common scenario—and that each particular combination of values is treated as an n-dimensional data point. If the task is relational, we know that particular outputs are contingent on relationships among the value combinations, and that outputs therefore should not be correlated with absolute values (coordinates) in any way. Data points associated with the same output should not share coordinates and therefore should *not* cluster together. If, on the other hand, the task is nonrelational, absolute values (data point coordinates) are associated with particular outputs; thus data points should tend to share coordinates and to cluster together.

In a relational task, then, we expect the data to show *no clustering*. And certainly, in extreme cases, this is precisely what is found. Consider the "parity task." In a parity task, the output and all the data values are represented as binary digits. The nature of the task is such that the result 1 should be produced just in case there is an odd number of 1's in the input, the result 0 being produced in all other cases. A parity task involving combinations of three data values can be written out textually as follows.

```
0  0  0  -->  0
0  0  1  -->  1
0  1  0  -->  1
0  1  1  -->  0
1  0  0  -->  1
1  0  1  -->  0
1  1  0  -->  0
1  1  1  -->  1
```

Each line above shows the association between a particular output (to the right of the arrow) and a combination of three input values (to the left). Note how the output is 0 in those cases where there is an even number of 1's among the input values, and 1 otherwise.

Parity is a *perfectly* relational task since the output depends *exclusively* on a relationship embracing *all* the input values. The net effect is that the distribution of data points is perfectly unclustered. Due to the nature of the parity rule, a single increment or decrement of any data variable flips the associated output from 1 to 0, or vice versa. Thus, in the input space, data points associated with a 1 output always appear *adjacent* to data points with the opposite output. Nearest neighbors within the space are thus guaranteed to have different outputs. There is no clustering whatsoever, and the output labels create a perfect checkerboard effect.

With respect to the parity tasks, the association between lack of clustering and relationality is thus quite clear and exactly as expected. But when we turn attention to other sorts of relational tasks, the association becomes more blurred. Consider, for example, the following task.

```
3  4  -->  0
8  2  -->  1
7  6  -->  1
8  9  -->  0
```

The rule here is that the output should be 1 just in case the first input value is greater than the second. This rule is characteristically relational, and we might expect that the problem—like parity—will exhibit no clustering. But if we inspect the associated distribution of data points, we find that this is not the case. The task is *less* than perfectly relational since

```
c d a b --> f
a b d b --> h
e c d e --> h
c b a e --> f
a c d e --> f
b c a e --> f
b d d e --> h
e d a c --> f
a c d c --> h
c d a c --> h
```

Figure 7.2
Hybrid learning task

outputs do not depend exclusively on relationships among the data. Absolute values do have some significance in the determination of output. Zero, for example, cannot be greater than any other nonnegative integer. A 0 as the first value is evidence that the produced output should be 0. The net effect is that the data for this task do show a degree of clustering.

Characteristically relational problems, then, may embody nonrelational aspects that "show through" in the form of clustering. But this is not the only source of clustering effects we need to consider. It is also possible for a task to be characteristically *hybrid*, that is, to exhibit different associations based on totally unrelated types of effects. For example, consider the problem in figure 7.2.

Inspection will reveal that there exists a cluster of points which share *a* in the third variable and *f* as output. A learner observing this effect might classify the problem as nonrelational and attempt to find input/output associations based solely on absolute values. This might lead to the prediction that a value of *a* in the third variable *indicates* the output should be *f*. But the original classification here is dubious. In addition to the effect noted, there is also an effect in which cases exhibiting *duplicated* data values tend to have *h* as their output. This effect is based on a relationship among the data. A learner focusing on this property might classify the problem as relational and proceed to a totally different conclusion.

We have to conclude, then, that clustering—or lack of it—is a less than totally reliable indicator for relationality. There are a number of possible sources of clustering in (the data for) a characteristically relational problem.

• The task may have genuine, nonrelational aspects and thus exhibit a degree of meaningful clustering. (The "greater-than" task is a good example.)
• The task may be represented to the learner in such a way as to create artificial nonrelational aspects. An example of this situation is a parity task whose representation includes an extra input variable whose value simply records the parity status of the original inputs.

In both of these situations, the exhibited clustering is useful for the purposes of learning since it can be used as the basis for prediction. There are two further situations, however, in which the clustering is of *no* use whatsoever.

• The clusters may be an artifact of the way in which the learner's data have been selected or generated.
• The clusters may be the results of some sort of noise or data error.

In these cases, the clusters observed in the data are sampling artifacts and thus of no use whatsoever within the learning process.

To summarize, in a characteristically relational task we may see clustering effects arising from nonrelational aspects of the task, characteristics of the task encoding, characteristics of the data selection process, or noise/error. Effects due to the task encoding, data selection, or noise may be termed *incidental*, on the grounds that their relationship to the underlying problem is not meaningful. Within this grouping, effects due to characteristics of the task representation may be termed *generalizing*, while effects due to data selection or noise may be termed *nongeneralizing*. The various possibilities are tabulated in figure 7.3.

7.6 Geometric Separability

But let us not get carried away with caveats. Despite the difficulties noted, it remains the case that nonrelationality *tends to* produce clustering and relationality *tends to* eliminate it. The existence or lack of clustering therefore can serve as a guide for classification decisions. The basic rule is that the more clustering a problem exhibits, the more probable a

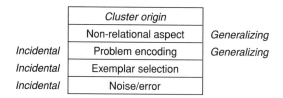

	Cluster origin	
	Non-relational aspect	*Generalizing*
Incidental	Problem encoding	*Generalizing*
Incidental	Exemplar selection	
Incidental	Noise/error	

Figure 7.3
Cluster origins in a characteristically relational problem

nonrelational classification. But to apply such (tentative) classification decisions based on evidence of clustering, we obviously need a measurement method.

Among the many approaches that might be taken, I have found an effective strategy to be the measurement of *geometric separability (GS)*[3] The geometric separability of a particular supervised-learning problem (input/output mapping) is just the proportion of data points whose nearest neighbors share the same output. The definition may be written formulaically thus:

$$GS(f) = \frac{\sum_{i=1}^{n} f(x_i) + f(x_i') + 1 \bmod 2}{n}.$$

Here $GS(f)$ is the geometric separability of binary target function f, x is the data set, x_i' is the nearest neighbor of x_i, and n is the total number of data.

Geometric separability is primarily a measure of the degree to which data points with the same output cluster together. But in some sense, it is also a generalization of the *linear separability* concept.[4] Although not a Boolean measure (i.e., a predicate), geometric separability can be viewed, like linear separability, as differentiating tasks that are appropriate for a particular learning strategy.[5] The strategy in this case is nonrelational (similarity-based) learning. Only if the geometric separability for a particular task is high is this strategy likely to be effective.

In chapter 5, the proportion of output-sharing nearest neighbors—the value we are now terming geometric separability—was shown to be the *expected* generalization performance for the 1-NN learner. We have thus pressed the GS measure into double service. But there is no conflict. Geometric separability is rightly seen as serving a dual role. On the one hand, it is an indicator of the degree to which nonrelational learning may succeed. On the other, it is the expected generalization performance of the 1-NN learner. The interesting implication is that, in some sense, the 1-NN method distills the essence of nonrelational, similarity-based learning.

7.7 Alignment and Salience

We have been concentrating in this chapter on the formal aspects of learning. But it is worth remembering that in the real world, the process of learning is something that is carried out by a particular learner agent with the aim not of solving an abstract problem, but of achieving a particular type of behavior. The learner agent can be expected to have some sort of sensory equipment producing sensory signals (i.e., inputs) and some sort of motor equipment producing motor outputs (i.e., behavior). We can further assume that the sensory mechanisms are "tuned" in a particular way and will respond to particular types of phenomena, that is, different properties and objects of the environment. But since not all sensors respond to all phenomena, there are a number of relationships a particular sensory mechanism S may have with some particular phenomenon P. These can be characterized in terms of variations in sensor *alignment*:

• Perfect alignment: S explicitly measures or detects P, that is, signals from S correspond directly to states of P.
• Perfect nonalignment: S does not respond to P in any way.
• Partial alignment: P has an indirect impact on S, that is, signals from S are affected by states of P but not in any direct, 1-to-1 way.

To illustrate these cases, imagine that we have a robot equipped with a light sensor whose signals vary monotonically with the amount of light arriving at the sensor surface. With respect to the phenomenon of "light intensity," the sensor is perfectly aligned. With respect to the phenomenon of "wind speed," the sensor is perfectly nonaligned. And with respect to the phenomenon of "season" (whether it is currently summer, spring, or winter), the sensor has to be considered partially aligned, since signals from the light sensor reflect the season to some degree, although not in any simple, 1-to-1 way.

Now consider an obstacle sensor. This is perfectly aligned with respect to obstacles, perfectly nonaligned with respect to light, and partially aligned with respect to car traffic.[6]

For a given behavior (i.e., learning problem), some properties and objects of the environment are salient and some are not. With respect to a feeding behavior, food may be salient but sand is probably not. With respect to tightrope-walking, gravity is probably salient but UV radiation is probably not.

If, in a particular learning scenario, a sensor is perfectly aligned with a phenomenon that is salient for the target behavior, then particular signals from that sensor will tend to be associated with particular outputs. In geometric terms, this means that all the inputs which exhibit particular input values (e.g., are in the same "row" of the relevant sensory space) will all have the same output label. In a two-dimensional sensory space, if both sensors are perfectly aligned with salient phenomena, data points with the same label will necessarily appear to *cluster*.

Learning methods that rely on clustering effects—fence-and-fill methods—are thus *guaranteed* to succeed if utilized sensors are perfectly aligned with salient phenomena. If the sensors are only partially aligned, clustering is unlikely and fence-and-fill methods are not guaranteed to succeed. (If the sensors are perfectly *non*aligned, then *any* learning method should fail, since it is attempting to operate without *any* salient information.) Application of the fence-and-fill strategy in the context of realistic, behavior-producing learning agents therefore seems to require the utilization of perfectly aligned sensors.[7] But this presents us with some serious problems.

Let's say that our aim is the construction of viable artificial agents (i.e., useful robots). Such agents need to be able to learn *many* behaviors that are likely to be contingent upon a *wide* range of phenomena. If we are committed to the use of fence-and-fill methods, we face the prospect of having to equip such agents with large numbers of perfectly aligned sensors—a new sensor set, in fact, for each distinct behavior. Consider the way in which this will lead to runaway sensory requirements.

- Learning how to deliver mail requires a mailbox sensor.
- Learning how to shoot down balloons requires a balloon sensor.
- Learning how to switch lanes on the highway requires a fast-lane detector.
- Learning how to put sugar in coffee requires a cup-top detector.

When learning is targeted at realistically high-level tasks, the requirement for perfectly aligned sensory input begins to look unsustainable. To satisfy it, we must work out, on a task-by-task basis, which properties of the environment are salient for which task, and then provide the agent with sensory equipment that measures or detects each and all of those properties. If we want to provide our agent with even a limited degree of generality, this approach will lead to the generation of a patchwork quilt of overspecialized sensory surfaces.

Where our aim is to explain the learning processes of natural agents, we encounter a still more severe variation of the same problem. Nature tends to exploit general-purpose sensory mechanisms (vision, audition, olfaction, etc.) that tend to be partially aligned with a wide range of salient phenomena. Thus explanatory models that rely on the utilization of perfectly aligned sensors appear to have little hope of generic application.

The net effect is that any learning scenario which assumes a learning agent equipped with perfectly aligned sensors should really be considered a "toy model," and any problem with high geometric separability should have a label attached reading Beginners Only. Nobody should (be allowed to) make the mistake of thinking that such scenarios are technologically challenging. Importing perfectly aligned sensors is generally a "fix" that trivializes the problem at hand, guaranteeing a quick solution by any reasonable fence-and-fill method.

The bottom line in learning-problem complexity, then, is just this:

- Perfectly aligned sensors imply *easy*.
- Partially aligned sensors imply *hard*.

But, paradoxically, the difficulty of learning problems is often judged in a quite different way. In fact, within the machine-learning literature, learning problems tend to be rated according to their *context*. A problem will typically be viewed as challenging if it has been derived from the "real world," and easy otherwise. Artificial-learning problems—like learning to do addition—thus tend to be considered easy, while "real world" problems—like learning to diagnose plant diseases—tend to be considered hard.[8]

The reality, however, is that these complexity assessments are often quite at odds with the facts. Rarely does the difficulty of a problem have anything to do with its context. A problem involving something that seems easy to us—like learning to distinguish even from odd numbers—may be utterly intractable to a fence-and-fill learner. Conversely, a problem that seems to us rather difficult—like learning to distinguish states of a jet engine likely to lead to failure—may be trivial. It all depends on how the inputs are presented, that is, what assumptions are made about the alignment of the learner's sensory mechanisms. It is just as the computer scientists always told us: representation is *key*.

7.8 Sensation Entropy

The requirement for generality seems to dictate that realistic agents must use lower-level sensory mechanisms. But the price of making sensors more primitive is a loss of alignment, since the higher-level, macroscopic aspects of the world with which the learning agent is naturally concerned are then apparent to the learner only in the form of relational effects. There thus seems to be a fundamental trade-off between generality and alignment. Increasing generality means decreasing alignment. In effect, generality can be "purchased" at the cost of decreased alignment and vice versa.

Nature appears to have negotiated this trade-off differently for different species. Consider, for example, the whirligig beetle. Such beetles, which are found on the surface of still ponds and lakes, engage in a continuous and rapid rotational movement, the aim being to confuse potential predators. The primary sensory mechanism of the whirligig beetle is a divided antenna that rests partly on and partly above the water. Using this antenna, the beetle senses the movements of nearby objects (including itself) by detecting the ripples created on the surface of the water. The whirligig beetle thus uses a "ripple detector" to sense salient phenomena in its environment.

But note how the beetle's ripple sensor is aligned with a much narrower range of natural phenomena than is, say, the ear of a chimpanzee. The ripple sensor responds directly (in a perfectly aligned way) to various forms of salient macroscopic phenomena (e.g., arrival of predators). It thus samples reality at a higher level, which facilitates a learning process of lower complexity. But there is a price to be paid in terms of generality: the ripple detector will never be of any use in detecting the presence of airborne predators, for example.[9]

This trade-off theory suggests that we can see learning as clawing back alignment in the wake of a generality "spending spree." Movement in the direction of generality effectively decreases the order of sensory stimuli by increasing what we might term *sensation entropy*. The role of learning is then to reverse the trend and reduce such entropy to manageable levels. The end result is a system with a greater level of generality but the *same* level of alignment, that is, a system which is cognitively enhanced. Cognitive development through evolution might therefore be viewed as a balancing act that aims to synchronize upstream, sensory operations with downstream, signal-processing operations, while at the same time pushing both to ever higher levels of sophistication.

7.9 Notes

1. This argument slightly glosses the truth. There is a special case in which we may have an implicit regularity involving values of a single variable. In this case, of course, we would not normally talk about the property in terms of a "relationship."

2. In recent years this subfield has become closely associated with the practice of *inductive logic programming*. See Muggleton (1992).

3. I first introduced this measure as the "geometric separability index" in Thornton (1997).

4. Minsky and Papert (1988).

5. A satisfying property of geometric separability is the fact that it is 0 for all parity tasks, as per expectation.

6. A partially aligned sensory signal might seem to be much the same as a noisy signal. But the alignment classifications should be viewed as defined in terms of noiseless signals. Noise has no significance within the taxonomy.

7. In classical machine learning, this is sometimes expressed by saying that empirical learning methods work well if and only if a suitable input representation is used (Dietterich et al. 1982).

8. For an example of this line of reasoning, see Holte (1993).

9. Another intriguing example of the natural occurrence of a perfectly aligned sensor appears to be the cricket ear. See Webb (1994).

8

The Supercharged Learner

The secret of creativity is knowing how to hide your sources.
Albert Einstein

8.1 The Relational/Nonrelational Continuum

In the previous chapter we saw that data regularities may appear in a
nonrelational or a relational form. In the former case, discovery is a finite
process that can be accomplished by a fence-and-fill method. In the latter
case, exploitation involves dealing with the space of possible relationships. And since this is, in general, *infinitely* large, relational learning is,
in principle, an infinitely hard operation. The outlook for learning is thus
a contingent issue that begins to seem rather sterile. Nonrelational
learning verges on the trivial. Relational learning begins to look like it
may be out of the question for all practical purposes.

But there are reasons to be cheerful. As hinted in the previous chapter,
there are ways of approaching the task of relational learning that turn
out to be reasonably effective in practice. The key idea to bear in mind
is that it is only parity-like mappings which create perfectly relational
scenarios. All other relational problems tend to have one foot in the
nonrelational camp, that is, they tend to exhibit a mixture of relational
and nonrelational effects. Most problems are thus situated somewhere
between the perfectly relational and the perfectly nonrelational scenarios.

A useful picture to have in mind is that of figure 8.1. This picks out
some sample points along the relational/nonrelational continuum. Each
rectangle represents a problem in the familiar form of a two-dimensional
graph. Each problem is assumed to be defined in terms of two numeric

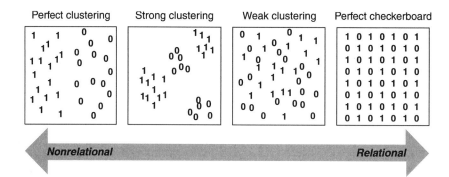

Figure 8.1
Clustering scenarios

input variables and one output variable, whose value is either 1 or 0. The problems represent typical scenarios from the perfectly nonrelational to the perfectly relational.

In the "perfect clustering" scenario, all the inputs whose output label is 1 are in the left half of the input space. Inputs with the output label 0 are in the right half of the space. The data are thus perfectly organized into two cleanly separated regions, definable in terms of a single axis-aligned boundary.

Next, we have a scenario showing strong clustering. The inputs here are still cleanly separated into uniformly instantiated regions. But the organization is less clean. The clusters would need to be defined in terms of, say, four circular regions.

The next scenario shows weak clustering. Now the input points are distributed in a more complex fashion. There are some uniformly instantiated regions, but these do not have particularly regular shapes. The situation might correspond to a characteristically relational problem that shows some nonrelational effects. Or it might simply correspond to a complex nonrelational problem.

Finally, we have the checkerboard scenario. In this situation the two types of input are perfectly mixed up. This is the extreme case of input data disorganization, that is, maximum sensation entropy. Every point has, as its nearest neighbor, a data point with a different label. Absolute input values (coordinates) have no significance *whatsoever* in the deter-

| 1 | 0 |
| 0 | 1 |

Figure 8.2
Checkerboard pattern for a parity problem

mination of output. Of course, *we* can see that the checkerboard data are highly organized. But the organization we perceive has to do with the relationships between the points. It has nothing to do with explicit commonalities, that is, nothing to do with absolute *position*.

The perfect checkerboard scenario forms the relational extreme on the clustering continuum. And clearly, there is no difficulty in drawing out such checkerboards and demonstrating that within the associated input/output mapping, absolute input values are not significant in the determination of the output label. But not all such scenarios constitute valid learning problems. How can we tell the difference between the ones that do and the ones that do not?

The parity mapping is, as ever, the place to begin. This is defined in terms of binary input and output values. And due to the underlying rule—which states that the output is 1 if the input contains an odd number of 1's, and 0 otherwise—nearest neighbors always have opposite outputs. Visually speaking, parity problems therefore *always* define perfect checkerboards. But since the input variables are all binary, each dimension of the input space has only two values. Thus, if we draw out the checkerboard for a two-bit parity problem, it has the rather dull appearance of figure 8.2.

Checkerboards whose dimensions are all two-valued can thus always be viewed as *n*-bit parity problems—*n* being the number of dimensions. Problems such as the one shown in figure 8.1, which have more than two values per dimension, but only two distinct output values, obviously cannot be interpreted as parity problems. However, they can be interpreted in terms of a modulus-addition operation, a generalization of the parity rule.[1] A mapping such as the one shown in figure 8.1 can be interpreted as defining a modulus-addition function using input values that range between 0 and 7 and a modulus value of 2.

In fact, *any* scenario that is checkerboard-like in terms of having different output labels attached to all nearest-neighbor data points, can be interpreted as defining a modulus-addition problem as long as the number of values in each dimension is a multiple of the modulus value. This is a simple consequence of the fact that within a modulus-addition operation, increasing or decreasing any input value *always* has the effect of changing the output value. The net effect is that within any modulus-addition mapping, nearest-neighbor data points always have *different* outputs. Any modulus-addition problem thus has a checkerboard-like appearance. By the same token, all problems with a checkerboard-like appearance can be viewed as modulus-addition problems.

8.2   Sneaky Problems

The perfect relationality of modulus-addition problems opens up a number of interesting possibilities. We can, for example, construct "sneaky" learning problems by taking a modulus-addition mapping and converting the numeric input/output values into symbolic values. The result is likely to be a problem that has the appearance of nonrelationality but that in fact is just as difficult for a fence-and-fill method as the standard parity problem.

The training pairs shown in figure 8.3 provide an illustrative example. The underlying mapping here is a modulus-addition problem using a modulus value of 2. The original binary output values have been translated into "yes" and "no" in the obvious way. And the input values have been translated into English words like "person," "consumes," and "heat" so as to produce a reasonably deceptive effect. The problem looks plausible. But if we feed a training sample of these data to a standard fence-and-fill method such as C4.5, we will obtain a generalization performance that is no better than random guessing.

Modulus-addition mappings also are useful when we want to illustrate how data sampling may create nongeneralizing incidental effects. Consider a modulus-addition mapping in which the modulus value is 2 and the input values range between 0 and 5. Plotting out the data points in the two-dimensional input space reveals the expected checkerboard pattern, as shown in figure 8.4(a). However, if we select a subset of these

```
person   consumes heat          --> yes
person   consumes electricity   --> no
person   consumes moisture      --> yes
person   consumes silicon       --> no
person   dislikes heat          --> no
person   dislikes electricity   --> yes
person   dislikes moisture      --> no
person   dislikes silicon       --> yes
computer consumes heat          --> no
computer consumes electricity   --> yes
computer consumes moisture      --> no
computer consumes silicon       --> yes
computer dislikes heat          --> yes
computer dislikes electricity   --> no
computer dislikes moisture      --> yes
computer dislikes silicon       --> no
```

Figure 8.3
Consumption problem based on mod-addition mapping

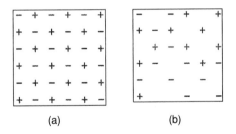

    (a)   (b)

Figure 8.4
Data points for modulus-addition problem

data for training purposes, we inevitably create some "holes." And, of course, when we have holes, we necessarily have clusters around the edges (see figure 8.4(b)). But the clustering here is a sampling artifact— an accidental consequence of the way in which the training data have been selected. It counts as a nongeneralizing incidental effect, and it therefore cannot form the basis for effective generalization.

8.3   Supercharging

The previous chapter noted that relational problems may show exploitable nonrelational effects, and that the application of fence-and-fill methods to relational problems may therefore produce acceptable results. However, we need to remember that the exploitable effects in the relational scenario are likely to be more complex than in the nonrelational case. To have any hope of successfully dealing with such situations, the fence-and-fill learner must be able to exploit a larger number of less well-defined clusters. There is a need, therefore, to increase the *power* of the fence-and-fill method—to endow it with the ability to separate out a messier configuration of regions.

Recall that the standard fence-and-fill method makes use of a limited number of simple bounding constructs to separate off uniformly instantiated regions. A simple way to increase power is thus to remove the constraint on the number of boundaries. Taking this to the limit, we may allow the utilization of an infinite number of boundaries. An alternative approach involves increasing the complexity of the bounding constructs available, that is, allowing the fence-and-fill method to manipulate and/ or create more sophisticated bounding surfaces.

A third possibility involves leaving the fence-and-fill method unchanged but applying a *sparsification* of the input data (by adding dimensions) so as to spread out the data points in the input space. This is a cunning approach since it involves operating exclusively on the data, and thus gives the impression of not affecting the learner in any way.

All these approaches involve spending resources in an attempt to increase the effectiveness of the fence-and-fill method in the relational realm. And in fact, all such methods are broadly equivalent. Increasing the number of simple bounding constructs that can be used can be viewed as a means of increasing the complexity of bounding surfaces. Similarly, increasing the dimensionality of the input space can be viewed as a means of providing a virtual enhancement to the boundary-creating abilities of the learner. All these approaches are essentially ways of "tuning up" the fence-and-fill regime. Here, they will be classified under the heading of *supercharged* fence-and-fill learning.

Hands-on v. Hands-off Supercharging Using Backpropagation

A natural vehicle for the supercharging approach is the multilayer perceptron (backpropagation) method, from chapter 4. The MLP is a neural-network method that, in its standard, two-layer variant, can be viewed as manipulating a composition of linear boundaries in the input space. The number of boundaries has to be decided in advance, and typically the number is fixed to some low value, thus consigning the method to the standard fence-and-fill category. However, the number of boundaries can be set arbitrarily high. And by increasing the number of boundaries (hidden units) we straightforwardly achieve a supercharging effect.

The drawback, of course, is that we *still* have to decide how many boundaries are to be used. Ideally, we would like the method to make up its own mind how many boundaries are needed. One way to achieve this, without moving outside the backpropagation scenario, involves using the *cascade-correlation* method.[2] This is a variation on the theme of backpropagation that adds in new boundary-defining hidden units on a unit-by-unit basis until the achieved performance on the training data is deemed satisfactory.

The method begins by training a minimal network, a process that continues until the error is no longer falling. A new unit is then added to the network, which takes input from all the original input units *and* any existing hidden units, and sends output to all output units. This unit is now trained independently to generate outputs that compensate for the existing error. The process is then continued until a network architecture is produced that generates an acceptably low level of error.

Virtual Supercharging: The MONKS2 Story

The cascade-correlation algorithm enables the MLP to "self-supercharge" by giving it the ability to create arbitrary numbers of boundary-defining units. And this is, in a sense, the obvious approach to take when trying to achieve the supercharging effect. But we should not neglect the other possibilities. The sparsification approach is certainly worth consideration. In this strategy we do not change the learning method in any way. Instead, we recode the data so as to represent the data points in a higher-dimensional input space. The general effect is to "spread out" the data. This has the effect of achieving a *virtual* enhancement of the boundary-making capabilities of any applied learner.

By increasing the dimensionality of the input space, we increase the probability that there will be a simple way of separating off any given group of points. Thus we effectively increase the power and flexibility of the (simple) bounding construct used. Of course, in increasing the dimensionality we inevitably increase processing costs. Sparsification is thus really feasible only with modestly sized training sets or very efficient fence-and-fill methods. If we are already at the limit of processing capabilities, input-data sparsification is not a realistic proposition.

There are a number of ways in which we can implement sparsification. A simple technique is *sparse coding*. This involves creating a recoding of the target mapping in which each variable in the recoded data records the presence of one *value* from the original encoding, as in figure 8.5.

An interesting demonstration of the power of virtual supercharging using sparse coding was provided in the MONKS competition, held in the early 1990s. In this event, machine-learning researchers from around the world applied popular learning methods to a number of benchmark generalization problems. One of these, the MONKS2 problem, involved a clearly relational input/output rule. This stated that the output should be true if "exactly two of the six [input variables] have their *first* value." All the input variables in this problem took scalar (i.e., sequence-based) values.

Given the relational nature of this rule, we expect to find relatively weak clustering[3] and to obtain poor performance from fence-and-fill learning. In the event, ID3, a standard fence-and-fill learner, *did* perform rather badly, but backpropagation produced perfect generalization performance (100% accuracy on the test sample). This performance was achieved by a *combination* of supercharging methods: first the number of available boundaries was set to a comparatively large number; second,

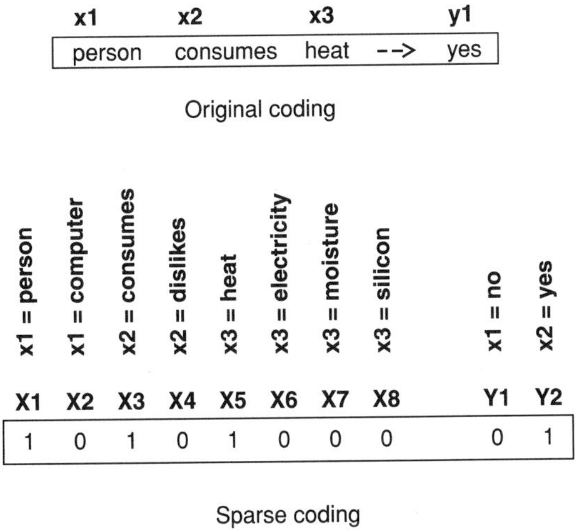

x1	x2	x3	y1
person	consumes	heat	-->	yes

Original coding

X1	X2	X3	X4	X5	X6	X7	X8		Y1	Y2
x1 = person	x1 = computer	x2 = consumes	x2 = dislikes	x3 = heat	x3 = electricity	x3 = moisture	x3 = silicon		x1 = no	x2 = yes
1	0	1	0	1	0	0	0		0	1

Sparse coding

Figure 8.5
Derivation of a sparse coding

a sparse coding was introduced that effectively inflated the input space from its original six-dimensional form to a seventeen-dimensional, binary-valued space.

Of course, all fence-and-fill methods benefit from sparse coding, provided the additional data-processing burden is acceptable. Thus, we can, if we like, improve the performance of ID3 on the MONKS2 data by the same method. In the competition, the reported generalization was 67.9%.[4] But if we apply ID3 to the data encoded in the seventeen-dimensional form, the performance improves by nearly 10%.

Noise and the Problem of Overfitting
In supercharging a fence-and-fill method, we provide it with the means of going further in the exploitation of clusters. But we need to make sure the method does not respond by going "over the top." As we have seen, realistic data are likely to exhibit some combination of exploitable effects (nonrelational effects or generalizing incidental effects) and nonexploitable effects (noise and data-sampling effects). In normal circumstances, the former are likely to be more pronounced than the latter. Thus, a

supercharged fence-and-fill method will naturally tend to exploit them first. But if processing is continued long enough, the method will eventually get around to exploiting the nongeneralizing effects. At this point, performance will begin to deteriorate. If we look at the generalization performance over the entire cycle of processing, we see an initial improvement followed by a deterioration. In this situation, the learner is said to *overfit* the data.[5]

A natural approach to the problem of overfitting involves watching how the generalization performance changes over time and trying to spot the moment at which the deterioration sets in. But it can be hard to distinguish natural oscillations in generalization from the effects of overfitting. In practice, the problem is often addressed simply by imposing some upper limit on the resources available to the learner, that is, by limiting the degree of supercharging.

8.4   The Need for Relational Partitions

The use of supercharged fence-and-fill methods on relational problems may achieve reasonable levels of performance. But it is unlikely to produce perfect or even near-perfect generalization. The reasons should, by now, be obvious enough. In the relational scenario, only some forms of clustering support generalization. And in general, there is no way to tell up front the difference between forms that will and forms that will not. Thus the generalizations made by the supercharged fence-and-fill in the relational scenario tend to lack accuracy. A better approach is needed. But what?

To move beyond the supercharging approach, we need to think carefully about the nature of the challenge we are confronted with. The relational scenario poses a hard problem for the computational learner. But it is *not* hard because it offers no basis upon which to form generalizations. It is hard because the basis it offers is relational! This may seem tautological. But it is a key observation. The implication is that relational problems really need to be solved through identification of relevant relationships. The (supercharged) fence-and-fill method attempts to finesse the problem—to take advantage of the nonrelational properties offered. But a genuine solution should render unto Caesar that which is Caesar's.

It should seek to generalize relationships by determining what those relationships really are.

Of course, any learner that is able to identify relationships must have some knowledge of *possible* relationships. And this conjures up an image of a learner that is going to use knowledge of relationships to create knowledge of relationships—an apparently circular operation. But the circularity disappears when we see that the relationships in the two cases do not have to be the same. A learner might use certain known relationships to attempt to exploit certain *unknown* relationships. This is really much the same thing as a learner that uses certain bounding constructs to exploit some unknown configuration of clusters. And, indeed, in some sense a known relationship *is* a kind of "bounding construct." It does not bound points in any geometric or spatial sense. Rather, it defines a *selection*. Certain data points exhibit the relationship and are thus within the selection. Certain others are not. A relationship in this context is thus something like a nonspatial boundary. But in the context of relational learning—where clusters and boundaries have no real significance—a nonspatial boundary is exactly what is required.

In order to make this idea work in practice, we need to equip the learner with the means of utilizing certain known relationships in the same way that the similarity-based learner uses boundaries. This means we have to provide the learner with operational definitions for certain relationships, that is, the relationships in terms of which we expect the learner to solve the problem. For example, let us say the main relationship to be identified in solving a particular relational learning problem is that of "threshold." We might proceed by providing the learner with an operational definition of the "greater-than" relation, on the grounds that the concept of "threshold" can be partially defined in terms of this concept.

In doing this, we are effectively providing the learner with appropriate *background knowledge*. And the criticism might be made that this is tantamount to telling the learner the answer in advance. But there is really no difference between this approach and the one pursued in fence-and-fill learning. In both cases the learner is provided with the means of introducing appropriate partitions. It is just that in the nonrelational case the partitions are spatial boundaries, and in the relational case they are not.

8.5   Pick-and-Mix Learning and Kepler's Third Law

When we provide a learner with operational definitions of relationships, we effectively provide it with the means of picking out a selection of spatially distributed data points and treating them as if they all belong to the same set. A reasonable mnemonic for the strategy is thus *pick-and-mix* learning, the term that will be used from here on.

A classic example of the pick-and-mix strategy is provided by the BACON method.[6] In its usual configuration, BACON is provided with knowledge of certain primitive mathematical relationships. It then carries out a search through the space of possible compositions of those relationships, testing in each case to see the degree to which the mathematical construct predicts the presented data.

Using this methodology, the BACON program has achieved a number of successes, including the derivation of Kepler's third law of planetary motion (see chapter 3). Recall that Kepler's third law of planetary motion states that the squares of the periods of planets are proportional to the cubes of the mean radii of their orbits. In other words, it states that the square of the year is proportion to the cube of the average distance from the sun. If y represents the length of the planet's year and d represents the average distance from the sun, Kepler's third law states that $\frac{y^2}{d^3}$ is constant.

In "rediscovering" this law, BACON starts out with just the raw values of y and d. It then explores increasingly complex formulas that can be constructed by using these variables together with the division and multiplication operators. This search works effectively from left to right through the columns in table 8.1 until it comes across a column in which all the values are identical. This occurs, of course, when the formula being explored is equivalent to Kepler's third law.[7]

The inventors of the BACON method have created other versions of the program by varying the subset of mathematical relationships (operations) used. And, of course, provided the search space used is appropriately customized, the program is guaranteed to succeed, that is, to discover whatever law applies. However, the method is sensitive to noisy data and, depending how the search is organized, it may also be sensitive to the instantiation and ordering of variables.

Table 8.1
Planet data

Planet	y	d	y/d	$(y/d)/d$	$((y/d)/d)y$	$(((y/d)/d)y)/d$
Mercury	0.24	0.39	0.62	1.61	0.39	1.00
Venus	0.61	0.72	0.85	1.18	0.72	1.00
Earth	1.00	1.00	1.00	1.00	1.00	1.00
Mars	1.88	1.52	1.23	0.81	1.52	1.00
Ceres	4.60	2.77	1.66	0.60	2.76	1.00
Jupiter	11.86	5.20	2.28	0.44	5.20	1.00
Saturn	29.46	9.54	3.09	0.32	9.54	1.00
Uranus	84.01	19.19	4.38	0.23	19.17	1.00
Neptune	164.80	30.07	5.48	0.18	30.04	1.00
Pluto	248.40	39.52	6.29	0.16	39.51	1.00
T. Beta	680.00	77.22	8.81	0.11	77.55	1.00

The fundamental problem with the BACON approach is that it requires the search space to be configured so that the solution is obtainable. In practice, this means giving the program the right components (e.g., mathematical operations) to work with. When the aim is to make the program rediscover a known law, this is straightforwardly achieved. However, where the aim is to discover regularities of an unknown form, customization of the search space may be more challenging.

8.6 FOIL

A more recent variation on the pick-and-mix theme is the FOIL method, devised by Ross Quinlan.[8] FOIL operates within the concept-learning scenario, that is, a supervised-learning problem in which target outputs are either "yes" or "no." It assumes that all the positive cases exhibit some particular relationship R and that none of the negative cases do. It also assumes that the relationship can be described in terms of a clause in the Prolog programming language. It attempts to derive this clause by incrementally adding terms (literals) to the end of an initially bodyless clause. In doing this, it examines all the feasible ways of constructing a term from data in the current database. Its aim is always to add the term that best improves the accuracy of the current definition, that is, its tendency to cover positive cases and exclude negative ones.

FOIL uses an *information-gain* method similar to the one used in ID3 for deciding which term to add in a given case. It always chooses the term that maximally reduces the current uncertainty about whether an arbitrary example covered by the definition is positive. In other words, FOIL always *maximizes* the relative coverage of positive examples (i.e., maximizes the uniformity of the covered set of cases). FOIL also makes use of a number of subsidiary heuristics. For example, it carefully avoids adding literals containing all-new variables. The rule is that a new literal has to contain at least one variable already seen in the clause. FOIL is also careful not to generate a clause in such a way as to allow for infinite recursion.

8.7   Relational Dilemma

BACON and FOIL differ in certain respects. BACON searches for mathematical relationships in numeric data. FOIL searches for logical relationships in symbolic data. However, under the surface the methods are rather similar. They both rely on algorithmic search. And they both utilize background knowledge. And it is this that constitutes the problem. To achieve success with the BACON method, we must provide the *right* mathematical operators. To achieve success with the FOIL method, we must provide the *right* set of predicates. In simple cases this requirement may not present any difficulty. But in realistic scenarios it is often difficult to identify appropriate domain knowledge. After all, it is probably a *lack* of familiarity with the domain that has triggered the desire to use machine learning in the first place.

Pick-and-mix methods approach the relational scenario in the "approved" manner. They focus on, and seek to exploit, *relational* properties of the data. They do not attempt to finesse the problem by exploiting available shortcuts. But they do demand what is, in effect, a sneak preview of the solution. If this preview cannot be provided, the approach runs into the sand.

We seem to be caught, then, between a rock and a hard place. Supercharged fence-and-fill methods, which engage in a "heroic" attempt to spatialize intrinsically nonspatial phenomena, cannot be expected to deliver top levels of performance. Pick-and-mix methods, on the other hand, may be able to deliver excellent performance but rely on the assistance of a farsighted, if not omniscient, supervisor. Clearly, a better solution is wanted.

The final chapters of the book will explore one way we might try to break out of the dilemma. The aim will be to see what can be achieved by reconceptualizing the role of the fence-and-fill method. Conventionally, a fence-and-fill routine is viewed as an independent learning procedure—something that we can utilize directly on any learning problem we are confronted with. However, in the model to be developed, the fence-and-fill method will be recast in a subsidiary role and used on an incremental basis (in collaboration with a recoding operation) so as to gradually break down the problematic relational problem in easy stages. As we will see in chapter 11, this reworking of the fence-and-fill methodology promises to provide the sort of performance that we expect from a suitably configured pick-and-mix method without paying the price of the expert configuration. It also sets us up to make more detailed connections between learning and processes of creativity.

8.8 Warehouse Security Example—Third Installment

Before proceeding, we will look at a third installment of the warehouse security scenario explored in chapters 2 and 5. Recall that in the first installment, the company introduced a security alarm system based on a couple of heat sensors. The tendency of the system to generate false alarms as a result of object settling was eliminated by using an application of the nearest-neighbors method. In the second installment, the company began using robotic stacking machines. Because these were operative 24 hours a day, the alarm system as originally configured generated security alerts throughout the night. An application of the LVQ algorithm was then utilized to endow the system with the ability to discriminate genuine intruder movements from those of the stacking machines.

In this, the third installment, the company decides to extend the warehouse building, adding a number of new shelving units. Because of the location of the sensors, the new floor space is not covered by the existing alarm system and the integrity of the system is thus seriously compromised. Rather than adding new sensors, however, the company decides to utilize one of its robotic stacking machines as an "automated security guard." The idea is to attach a couple of heat sensors to the superstructure of one of the stacking machines and then program the machine to repeatedly execute a tour of inspection of the entire warehouse area.

The original idea is to utilize the same approach as in the second scenario—that is, LVQ applied to a training set of positive and negative examples. However, the performance that is achieved this way turns out to be *very* disappointing. Close examination of the training set reveals that the data have the appearance of being randomly distributed. There are no visible clusters and there is no obvious separation between positive and negative examples. There is thus nothing for the LVQ method (or any other fence-and-fill method) to latch onto.

The cause of the difficulty is, of course, that the alterations to the sensory configuration of the system have fundamentally changed the situation "seen" by the learner. Let us imagine that the two heat sensors are sited on the upper part of the superstructure of the automated security guard (henceforth "the robot"), with one sensor on the left and one on the right, and both facing outward, as shown in figure 8.6(a). The aim, as

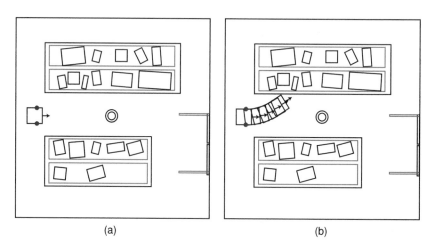

(a)   (b)

Figure 8.6
Warehouse plan with automated security guard

in previous scenarios, is that the system should be able to detect motion within the warehouse by looking at the differences between nearly simultaneous heat-sensor readings. But now there is the complication that some of the variations in the readings will be due to the motion of the *robot*. If the robot remains static, then there is, of course, no difficulty. The situation is exactly as before, only with differently positioned sensors. However, once the robot begins to move, there is an immediate impact on the heat-sensor readings. And this impact is distinct but not necessarily independent of the impact created by any moving object within the warehouse.

To begin with, let us focus on a simple case. Imagine that some source of heat (e.g., an animate object) is situated at the point marked by a double circle in figure 8.6(a). If the robot begins moving directly toward this source, then the heat-sensor readings will increase even if the source itself remains completely static. As long as the robot moves directly toward the source, the change will be the same for both sensors. The effect on the sensor data is thus *relational*. The changes caused within the data are instantiations of a particular relationship, namely, equality. Knowing what this relationship is enables one to predict one sensor reading from the other.

If the robot moves in a slightly different way, the effect may be altered. Imagine, for example, the effect that will be created if the robot rotates on the spot. Roughly speaking, as the robot rotates to the left from a head-on position, the readings from the left sensor will decrease while the readings from the right sensor will increase. The relational effect created in this case is quite different. The effect is that the *sum* of the values remains roughly constant.

If the robot exhibits both motions at once—see figure 8.6(b)—then the two distinct relational effects will be rendered simultaneously within the sensory data. But the effects are not independent; there is interference between them, and their instantiations within the data may therefore be difficult to disentangle.

If we know what the robot motions are, we can identify the relevant effects and discount them within the data. This should have the effect of returning the scenario to the original situation in which there is no robot motion to contend with. But of course, in general learning scenarios, we do not have this information. The learning problem we have created thus looks to involve dealing with relational effects. In other words, it looks as if the change we have made in the sensory configuration has moved the learning problem from the safe, nonrelational camp into the problematic relational camp.

The alignment concepts introduced in the previous chapter can help us here. When we take the sensors from the corners of the warehouse and site them on the robot, we eliminate their perfect alignment. In the original situation, the sensors directly measured the property that is significant for the prediction of output. But in resiting them, *perfect* alignment is exchanged for *partial* alignment. After the sensors have been repositioned, stimuli no longer directly "measure" the salient property of the environment. This property has an impact on the readings, but not in any 1-to-1 way. The motions of the robot now create interference.

Conceptualizing the effect in these terms reveals the symmetry that exists between a learner agent and its environment. From the learning agent's point of view, effects that are a result of the agent's behavior are *indistinguishable* from effects that are the result of dynamic properties of the environment. All partially aligned processes in the environment create relational effects in the learner's sensory data, regardless of their origins. But there is no need for learners to make any distinction between phenomena that are their own doing and phenomena that are outside their control. Rather, they can kill two birds with one stone by "pretending" there is no distinction to be made.

As Hendriks-Jansen has noted with respect to robotlike creatures, "The creature's morphology, its sensory-motor characteristics and the activity patterns it performs all affect its *Merkwelt*[9] and 'affordances,'[10] and consequently the 'problems' it has to 'solve.' Tasks, problems, and solutions to problems cannot be characterized independently."[11] On this view, the enterprise of relational learning may be visualized as a process directed both inward toward the learning agent's behavior and outward toward the environment. Relational effects then have a concrete but slightly counterintuitive basis: they are the sensory products of partially aligned phenomena[12] that may or may not be generated by the agent itself. But, whichever is the case, such effects always have a concrete origin; the process of relational learning is simply the attempt to reify it, that is, to provide it with an *instantiation*. Relational learning, then, may be viewed as a generic discovery operation—a procedure whose aim is to get access to currently inaccessible properties of the environment, *regardless* of their origin.

8.9 Notes

1. Modulus addition behaves just like ordinary addition except that the result is constrained to lie between 0 and a maximum called the *modulus* value. Applying modulus addition to some numbers involves finding their sum and then subtracting the modulus value M until the value lies between 0 and M-1.

2. Fahlman and Lebiere (1990).

3. Indeed, the organizers of the competition note that the MONKS2 problem is "similar to parity problems. It combines different attributes in a way which makes it complicated to describe in DNF or CNF" (Thrun et al. 1991).

4. Ibid.

5. The terminology is an import from the curve-fitting paradigm. Machine-learning researchers use the term *overtraining* to describe the same problem.

6. The BACON programs were developed by Langley and coworkers (Langley, 1978; Langley, 1979; Langley et al. 1983). BACON actually comes in several variants. Its cousins include GLAUBER, STAHL, and DALTON.

7. All values in the table are truncated to two decimal places.

8. Quinlan is also the inventor of the ID3 and C4.5 methods.

9. Von Uexkull (1957).

10. Gibson (1979).

11. Hendriks-Jansen (1996).

12. Typically such phenomena will be dynamic in some sense, but there is nothing in the argument that requires this.

9

David Hume and the Crash of '87

STOCKS PLUNGE 508 POINTS, A DROP OF 22.6%: 604 MILLION VOLUME NEARLY
DOUBLES RECORD.
New York Times, October 20, 1987

9.1 Ride a White Swan

Sometime on the morning of October 19, 1987, Michael Connor pulled
shut the door of his New York apartment and took the elevator to the
ground floor. In the lobby, the doorman gave him the customary nod and
inquired whether he needed a cab. The recent spate of commissions
meant that he could easily afford a cab ride downtown. But Connor
preferred to take the subway. It gave him time to think—to mentally
prepare for the day. He motioned "no" to the doorman and walked out
into the morning sun.

To reach the subway entrance, he had to walk a couple of blocks south
and, as usual, he planned to take a detour through the park. He didn't
feel the need to hurry. He had the pleasure of knowing that WHITESWAN
had automatically gone on-line at the start of trading. And given its typical productivity profile, he could expect to be able to show reasonable
profits without even being in his office. When he was actually there—
able to give the system the occasional nudge—the results could go way
up to the superleague. And all without setting hands on a phone. Connor
felt good.

A local train took him to Columbus Circle. Then it was just a few steps
across the platform to get the express. All in all, the ride took about
twenty minutes. Connor spent the time gazing into space, thinking about

the different things he could do with his rapidly accumulating wealth. His favorite dream was of cruising to the Carribean in a fifteen-berth schooner. But this morning he found himself thinking along more social lines. The concept of a penthouse party to celebrate his upcoming birthday had begun to get a grip on him. He made a mental note to start thinking about ways he could lay his hands on a suitable property.

When he arrived at the starkly furnished premises of B&B Investments, Connor made his way straight to his office. No point in pushing his luck too far, he decided. And, anyway, he could hardly wait to log on and see what the accumulation was since yesterday afternoon. He stepped inside his office and hung his jacket on the door peg, resisting the temptation to rush straight to the terminal. He flicked the double light switch and carefully adjusted the air conditioning. Only then did he walk calmly across the room and sit down on the low stool that he thought of as his "saddle."

The screen blared out in familiar lines of green and black. And almost at once Connor knew that something was wrong. The carefully designed WHITESWAN display was messed up along one side. An overflowing number field was pushing a column edge into an ugly zigzag. Connor sighed and thumbed a control sequence, switching from the main display to the numeric log. When the numbers flashed onto the display, he stared at them stupidly for more than a minute. He hunched over the screen, unable to take it in. And yet the figures were unambiguous. The "Michael index," as Connor liked to call the WHITESWAN internal profitability measure, was down 20 points. As he stared at the screen, it fell another point.

Connor felt something lurch inside him. He began flicking through the backlogs, cursing himself for not coming straight in to work. The data showed that the system had got itself into some sort of downward spiral. Almost from the opening of the market, WHITESWAN had been unloading onto falling prices, something that was *not* meant to happen. There'd been bears in the market for months. But this kind of drop was right out of a comic book. Connor picked up the phone and punched in a familiar number. Busy signal. He tried another. Also busy. He tried his secretary and got an announcement about "longer than usual" response times.

Moving to a second terminal, Connor started checking out the morning's trading. Screen after screen told the same story. Prices dropping like a stone. Going through the floor. Hitting the basement and still falling. No wonder WHITESWAN was in a spin. This kind of movement was way outside normal parameters. Connor pressed his hands into his eye sockets. He could feel the beginnings of something he dimly recognized as fear. Something weird was going on. But it had to be just a glitch. A trading hiccup. A readjustment. Just a short-term effect, he told himself. Something that would have self-corrected by lunchtime.

Unfortunately, Connor could not have been more wrong. It was 11 A.M. on October 19, 1987, a day later to become known as *Black Monday*. The worst stock market crash in history was unfolding across the stock exchanges of the world. Things were *already* very bad. But by the close of business, they would be a great deal worse.

Connor's day rapidly turned into an incomprehensible nightmare. For nearly an hour, he tried to tweak his system. He knew it was pointless. WHITESWAN was just doing what it was programmed to do—what every dealer was programmed to do—sell out if it looked like prices were going to fall. And prices were just hammering their way down like a space rocket in reverse. Nobody seemed to know what was happening. Phones were being allowed to ring, unanswered. People were running from room to room. The floor of the main office was littered with printouts. Pandemonium was setting in. But why? What was happening? Everyone knew the U.S. economy was in reasonable shape. A few ups, a few downs, but basically growth and more growth. Five full years of it. Everything functioning as it should. Confidence high. Consumer spending healthy. So why were the markets trying to replay the crash of '29?

Around midday, Connor got a call from the top floor. He was to get up there right away. Mr. Camilleri, B&B boss for the past fifteen years, wished to speak with him about "the situation." In the elevator, Connor found himself trying to remember the Lord's Prayer. The words just wouldn't come.

"We need a little explanation, here, Michael," said the deceptively diminutive Camilleri when Connor presented himself in the penthouse suite. "And we need it right now."

"Anything I can do, I'll do," said Connor, in what he hoped was a reassuring tone.

"You're not going to believe, this, Michael, but I've had people from the exchange phoning me all morning. They keep asking me if I know what's going on."

"Do we know?" asked Connor.

"That's what I want to know from you," boomed Camilleri. "All everyone keeps talking about is this program trading. Program trading this. Program trading that. What is this damn program trading, Michael? Is it some kind of computer thing? I want the details."

Connor spread out his hands, turned them face up. This was not what he had been expecting. "It's just a form of portfolio insurance, really."

"Don't try to goof me, Michael. Is it a computer thing?"

"Yes," admitted Connor. "It is a computer thing."

"You hook up the computer and the computer does the deals. Is that how it works?" Mr. Camilleri was clenching and unclenching his fists. "If you tell me it doesn't work like that, I'm going to have a problem. The NYSE thinks this is how it works."

"That's basically it. The computer just reacts the same way any one of us would react. It's nothing special."

"Are you using one of these systems, Michael?"

Could this be a rhetorical question? "I've ... dabbled," Connor admitted, white-faced.

"Well, you better start dabbling out, Michael, because there are people telling me that it's the program-trading computers that are pushing this bear into overdrive. I assume you've already switched your machine off. Am I right?" Mr Camilleri leaned forward menacingly.

"Well...."

"Is it off or is it on, Michael? We need to know."

Connor clenched his teeth. "Actually, it's still on."

"DAMN IT!" roared Camilleri. "You sonofabitch! Pick up that phone right now and have your secretary turn it off."

Connor did as he was bid, knowing full well that turning off the screen in his office wasn't going to make any difference. WHITESWAN was a remote task running on the mainframe in the basement. But it seemed unlikely that Mr. Camilleri would welcome this information.

As Connor gave his secretary detailed instructions for pushing the Off button on his terminal, Mr. Camilleri continued to rail. "I can't believe that something like this can go on here, without me knowing. It's unbelievable. These computer systems are supposed to be fail-safe. All this sh** about validation. It's not worth a damn when you get down to it."

Replacing the receiver, Connor noticed that his employer had stopped in midflow.

"Tell me, Michael," said Camilleri. "You did run your system through all the checks, didn't you? You did confirm that these deals it was going to be making were on the level?"

"Well...." Connor wondered whether this was a good moment to explain the technicalities of program trading. "When you make a deal, it's always going to be a kind of guess. There's no way of getting past that."

"But there are good guesses and bad guesses, Michael. I'd like you to tell me exactly what you did to prove that your system was going to be a good guesser."

"Well, I didn't actually try to prove that."

Mr. Camilleri smiled for the first time. It was not a pleasant expression. "I have a son, Michael. Did you know?"

"No," admitted Connor, "I didn't know."

"Well, no matter. This son of mine is an expert in computers. Did you know THAT?"

"No," admitted Connor, trembling. "I didn't know that."

"And this son of mine," continued Mr. Camilleri, into his stride now, "gives me all the latest news on the computer front. Do you know what he says the latest thing is?"

"Errm...."

"Let me tell you, Michael, since you plainly don't know. He says there are theories now that allow you to prove the CORRECTNESS of programs. So what I want to know is this, Michael. I want to know why you didn't prove the correctness of YOUR system. Take your time."

Connor let a few tense moments trickle by. But the thing had to be faced. "Mr. Camilleri, to explain this, er, technology, I need to start by asking you a question," said Connor.

"Ask away," growled Camilleri, placing his hands over his eyes.

"Have you heard of an 18th-century Scottish philosopher named David Hume?"

Camilleri's complexion darkened a shade. Newly riven furrows appeared around his ears and in the area above the bridge of his nose. His fists curled into compact balls and smashed down onto the leather surface of the king-size desk.

"Have I WHAT???"

9.2   The Problem with Science

October 19, 1987—Black Monday, as it is now known—was a particularly trying day for the those working in the U.S. financial sector. During the course of the day, the Dow Jones industrial average plummeted a full 508 points. This represented an unprecedented 23% drop in prices—more than double the fall that occurred during the 1929 crash. The global financial community was reduced to panic. But the market collapse did not come completely out of the blue: prices had been declining slowly for nearly two months, and on the Friday before the crash, the Dow Jones index had fallen by more than 100 points. Monday's collapse was on a scale that had simply never been experienced before. Traders, lulled into a false sense of security by the boom that had been ongoing since 1982, were taken by surprise.

But what caused the crash? At the time, as the Michael Connor story suggests, blame was placed on the use of program-trading systems, that is, systems like Connor's WHITESWAN. But why should these systems have been the target of suspicion?

Program-trading systems are computer programs that aim to reproduce the normal actions of an alert trader—buying securities whose value seems likely to increase and selling those whose value seems likely to depreciate. On the face of it, the utilization of such systems should make little difference to a market since they are simply replicating the actions of human traders. If anything, we might guess that they might improve stability a little. Computer programs are just machines and, as Mr. Camilleri himself noted, it is possible to test whether or not they work properly. The utilization of properly validated program-trading systems would appear to offer the prospect of *eliminating* human error.

But of course the problem with program-trading systems is not that they do not *work* properly. It is, rather, that the knowledge they use to make trading decisions is likely to be inadequate. This is the point that Connor was intending to make when he asked his boss whether he'd ever heard of David Hume. Hume is famous for having noted that all knowledge is derived from some sort of *inductive* process, that is, some sort of learning. Processes of this type, he observed, are essentially ways of using known properties of the world for making guesses about unknown properties. And since any guess is intrinsically uncertain, all knowledge must therefore be uncertain.[1]

Hume's assertion applies to all forms of knowledge, regardless of the form of representation. The rules inside a program-trading system are no exception—they are *necessarily* uncertain. Michael Connor's reference to Hume was just a preliminary move in an attempt to establish this point. Whether Camilleri would have been convinced, we can never know. But intuition suggests that his unhappiness would have been increased rather than ameliorated by the news that one of his employees was having a computer, using rules that were *guaranteed* uncertain, make deals on behalf of B&B clients.

And what would have happened if Connor had gone on to reveal the true scale of the problem? How would Mr. Camilleri have reacted to the news that the "guaranteed uncertain" label could be applied not only to the rules inside WHITESWAN but in fact to every single product of science and technology throughout the B&B building, including *all* the accounting and payroll systems, all the safety procedures, all the trading guidelines, the recipes followed by the cooks in the kitchens, the injection technology used by the engines in the courtesy limos in the parking lot, the fabric of the B&B building itself, and even the nut-and-bolt assembly responsible for stabilizing the spring-loaded recliner mechanism on Camilleri's $2,000 chair. Almost certainly, the news would have driven him close to the edge.

As for the question of the causes of the Black Monday crash, the jury is still out. Mr. Camilleri's confidence that program-trading systems were a root cause was widely shared. But it turns out that this explanation is, like the prior-warning story of the Coventry bombing, essentially a myth. Human traders naturally react to falling prices by selling stock. This tends to push prices down still further, triggering further rounds of selling. There is thus a natural feedback effect in all market trends. And in 1987 it was believed that because of the way program-trading systems focus more or less exclusively on price movements, they accentuate the effect, creating the potential for greater levels of instability.

However, in recent years, the theory has developed that although program trading may have contributed to the crash, it is unlikely to have been the sole cause. A range of factors have been identified that may have helped to push the market over the edge. Many observers have noted, for example, that stocks were significantly overvalued in the period leading up to the crash and that investors were adopting investment strategies which carried unprecedented levels of risk. The explanation may therefore involve a much broader range of factors than the story of Michael Connor suggests.[2]

9.3   Recovering from Hume's Crash

David Hume is sometimes viewed as a prophet of doom. His observations of the necessary uncertainty of knowledge seem to undermine the very idea of scientific progress. They also seem to suggest that methods of induction—learning by another name—can never be completely watertight. A natural gut reaction is to feel that there is little point in the enterprise of machine learning, since, according to Hume's argument, it can never fully achieve its goal. But such despair should be firmly resisted. While the results of an inductive process can never be considered certain, they may still be of considerable value. Furthermore, the *degree* to which they are of value can be formally measured (e.g., by testing predictive accuracy). Thus, the very tangible justification for investigating induction/learning is simply the requirement and desire to improve the efficacy of available methods.

So far in this book, we have focused exclusively on computational methods of learning developed within the last few decades. However, the investigation of induction has been going on a great deal longer. The philosophical literature on the topic stretches back to the Greeks. Aristotle, for example, talked about the process of *induction by enumeration*.[3] This is a similarity-based process in which we infer, for example, that since the first swan we see is white, the second swan we see is white, and the third swan we see is white, *all* swans must be white.[4] In general, induction was held by Aristotle to be any argument that was persuasive without being strictly deductive.

Francis Bacon, a contemporary of Kepler, tried to improve on the concept of induction by enumeration. He suggested that inductively derived generalizations could be checked through a search for "negative instances," foreshadowing the concept-learning paradigm that offers generalization through the combined use of positive and negative instances. In general, Bacon adopted a practical and objective outlook. For example, he attempted to draw attention to the way in which *idola mentis* (idols of the mind) can get in the way of objective scientific inquiry. (This argument, which appears in book I of the *Novum organum*, might almost have been directed at Kepler and his fascination with his spheres theory of the solar system.) However, it is thought that his familiarity with the day-to-day methods of his scientific contemporaries was limited.

Nearly 200 years later, John Stuart Mill attempted to refine the concept of induction still further. Mill proposed four "methods of scientific inquiry." These focused on the task of identifying causes within scientific data.[5] However, his concept of "cause" is close to what we are now calling "regularity," so his proposals are highly relevant. In fact, he proposed five rules of induction. The first reads "If two or more instances of the phenomenon under investigation have only one circumstance in common, the circumstance in which alone all instances agree is the cause (or effect) of the given phenomenon." In focusing on the role of similarity, this rule foreshadows the similarity-oriented learning methods already described. In fact, four of out of Mill's five rules emphasize the significance of similarity.

Closer to our own time, the philosopher Bertrand Russell wrote:[6]

The principle we are examining may be called the principle of induction, and its two parts may be stated as follows:

(a) When a thing of a certain sort A has been found to be associated with a thing of a certain other sort B, and has never been found dissociated from a thing of the sort B, the greater the number of cases in which A and B have been associated, the greater is the probability that they will be associated in a fresh case in which one of them is known to be present;

(b) Under the same circumstances, a sufficient number of cases of association will make the probability of a fresh association nearly a certainty, and will make it approach certainty without limit.

In this statement, Russell puts the spotlight on the process of *association*. But his proposal can be read as stating that the inductive process involves exploitation of *commonalities* among objects. As such, it is simply a new variation on the theory that sees induction as a process involving the exploitation of similarity.

9.4 Scandalous Philosophers

The writings of Russell, Bacon, Mill, and others paint a plausible picture of the way in which induction may be pursued. It is, moreover, a picture with a clear link to the similarity-based orientation of machine learning. However, there is nothing in any of this work—philosophical or computational—that has the slightest effect on the arguments of David Hume. Hume's observation that science's utilization of induction—the prediction of the unknown—inevitably produces uncertainty is totally unaffected by theories about how induction works. Science is thus left to languish in a low-status limbo, with little to save it from being lumped with witchcraft and mysticism.[7]

In the 20th century a proposal has been put forward by Karl Popper that offers the promise of a solution. Popper's approach is novel in that he does not attempt to quibble with the observation that inductively derived laws can never be deemed certain. Rather, he proposes to change the order of battle—to have the inductive process carried out in reverse. Popper argues that since confirmation of inductively derived theories and laws is out of the question, science should proceed by focusing on *refutation*. A single counterexample is sufficient to falsify a theory with absolute certainty. Science can therefore build secure foundations by accumulating *falsifications*. The methodological implications follow automatically: respectable scientists should attempt to select new theories according to their degree of falsifiability rather than according to their degree of plausibility.

Unfortunately, although Popper's scheme has a certain zany appeal, it is not entirely practical. If we take his proposal literally, there is nothing to prevent us—as scientists—from selecting a long sequence of incorrect theories. Provided each theory is falsifiable, we are proceeding in an entirely proper, Popperian manner. But the net effect is, of course, that no real progress is ever made.

9.5 Abolition of the Free Lunch

Where does all this leave us with respect to machine learning? To what extent do Hume's observations about uncertainty damage the credibility of computational-learning methods? Should we deem the project of machine learning to be theoretically doomed and not worth pursuing? Or are we justified in putting Hume's observations aside and carrying on as normal? The issue turns out to be surprisingly complex. It has recently formed the focus of a lively electronic debate among practitioners and theoreticians concerned with learning. Not all of the propositions advanced in this debate are of interest to us here. But some are worthy of a *brief* review.

The key positions that have been adopted are illustrated in the following (imaginary) courtroom debate between a "Prosecution" whose aim is to discredit inductive methods, and a "Defense" whose aim is to validate them. (Readers desiring exposure to the nonimaginary sources of inspiration should turn attention to the relevant Internet resources.)

Prosecution: It has been established since the early 18th century that the process commonly known as induction offers the practitioner no certainty in its results. The Prosecution respectfully suggests that Your Honor rule its practice unlawful, and ban it with immediate effect.

Defense: We emphatically reject the Prosecution's claim, Your Honor. The view of the Defense is that the problem of certainty in induction is irrelevant since the purpose of the method can be conceptualized purely in terms of probability maximization. The Defense therefore does not accept that there is any justification for a ban.

Prosecution: The position of the Defense on this issue was anticipated. The Prosecution has therefore prepared certain formal arguments that

Your Honor may find illuminating. May Exhibit A be presented to the court? [A paper resembling figure 1.2 is circulated.] Thank you. This, Your Honor, is a simple induction problem, known to practitioners as a concept-learning problem. It is, as you will see, a set of descriptions with attached classifications—in this case, the classifications being merely the labels "yes" and "no." As will be noted, the set is divided into halves. The first half is termed the training set; the second, the testing set. To solve the problem, it is necessary to induce a rule enabling the correct classification of descriptions in the testing set, solely on the basis of observations made on the training set. Would Your Honor care to attempt the task? [no answer]

In that case, I will continue. Proponents of induction would argue that methods may be brought to bear which will induce a satisfactory rule. However, it is easily shown that no such method can succeed in general, and by implication that induction is a vacuous exercise which should be outlawed. Note that we may take any given testing set, such as the one shown in exhibit A, and form its complement merely by reversing all the attached classifications, that is, by exchanging every "yes" for "no" and every "no" for "yes." Now, let us imagine that some particular inductive method induces a rule from the training set which leads to a proportion p of cases in the original testing set being correctly classified. Clearly, the proportion of cases that will be correctly classified in the complement of the testing set must be $(1 - p)$.

Now, every testing set has a complement. Thus an inductive method tested on all the problems from a particular class will encounter complements exactly half of the time. Its average performance will thus be the mean of p and $(1 - p)$, which, regardless of the value of p, is always 0.5. The conclusion, as Your Honor will no doubt have anticipated, is that the performance of any inductive method tested on *all* the problems from a class can be no better than 50/50, that is, no better than achieved by a man making classifications purely *at random*. The ineluctable conclusion is that induction methods are a sham and the investment of public resources in their investigation is a waste of money that should be curtailed forthwith.[8]

Defense: With all due respect to my learned friend, this argument is mere sophistry. He proposes that induction methods should be tested on *all* the problems which may be defined in a particular domain. But were we to do this, we would effectively be presenting the induction method with contradictory information. In order to produce better-than-random performance on both a problem and its complement, an induction method must behave inconsistently. It must produce different classifications for the same information at different times! My learned friend's argument is based on the assumption that induction methods are presented with what is in effect an impossible task. The conclusions that supposedly follow are therefore without substance.

Prosecution: I regret to say, Your Honor, that my learned friend appears to have misunderstood the nature of the argument that has been made. The point of the argument is not that induction methods are to be tested on *all* the problems from a given domain, merely that in practice we do not know in advance which particular problems in a domain will be encountered. I have established, I trust, that whenever the performance of an induction method on a particular problem is a certain degree above the 50/50 level, then it must be the same degree *below* the 50/50 level on the problem's complement. I would imagine that it is perfectly clear to any rational being that if we do not know which particular set of problems will be exhibited by a particular domain, then we have to assume that a method will encounter "originals" and "complements" in equal proportions, and therefore that our inductive method will produce average performance which is exactly at the 50/50 level.

Defense: Your Honor, I must object....

Prosecution: If I may be allowed to complete the point I was making....

[incoherent mutterings from the JUDGE]

Thank you. The point the argument seeks to make, Your Honor, is a subtle one. As I have noted, in the case where we do not know in advance which problems a method will encounter, we have no option but to assume that complements and originals will be encountered in equal proportions. By implication, it is the a priori knowledge that we bring to a domain which enables us to raise the performance of an induction method above the level of the random guesser. An induction method pitched into battle with only its internal resources to hand, inevitably produces performance that is without value. Performance above this level can be elicited only by throwing into the ring our own accumulated knowledge. In the scenario so tirelessly investigated by academic practitioners, the induction process itself thus plays *no role whatsoever*. The Prosecution therefore continues to respectfully request that Your Honor introduce measures to eradicate the process as a topic of publicly funded investigation.

Defense: The Defense welcomes the clarification that the Prosecution has now offered. However, Your Honor should note that, once again, conclusions are drawn which are in no sense justified. Counsel for the Prosecution would have us believe that inductive methods are without value on the grounds that their effective application requires the introduction of assumptions. But this is simply absurd. It is an article of faith throughout the scientific world that observation cannot take place in a vacuum. All processes of investigation are, to some degree, theory-laden and assumption-driven. The requirement, in the inductive scenario, for the introduction of effective assumptions—a point upon which my learned friend and I are in perfect agreement—is thus the normal requirement for *any* coherent scientific or technological procedure.

Prosecution: Apparently, Counsel for the Defense is beginning to appreciate the logic of our position. The efficacy of induction, it is now conceded, does depend crucially on the quality of background assumptions that are applied. However, while the Defense appears to believe that this somehow exonerates the practitioners of the art, the Prosecution continues to assert that the process is a sham. To reveal the paper-thin nature of my learned friend's position, one has only to ask how these assumptions—that we are all agreed are essential—are to be derived.

Defense: [nervously] I regret I am not completely familiar with the day-to-day procedures of the inductive practitioner, Your Honor. However, I believe it to be the case that, over the years, certain fundamentals have been established which are generally found to be effective in application. For example, it is widely recognized that similarity may play....

Prosecution: [leaping to his feet] The Prosecution *strongly* objects to this line of reasoning, Your Honor. Counsel for the Defense is using a circular argument in which he would have us believe that the products of one inductive process may be used as the basis for guaranteeing the efficacy of another. Should he continue with this stratagem, the court may find itself embroiled in an infinite regress.

Judge: [after a lengthy silence] I find these arguments extremely confusing and wish to hear no more of them. It does appear to me that Counsel for the Prosecution has the edge on it. I will therefore order steps to be taken to ensure that all practitioners and researchers of the so-called inductive method are brought to account....

9.6 Escape Clause

Fortunately, judges are notoriously unreliable. And we can safely assume that the investigation of induction and learning will continue to be lawful for the foreseeable future. But the fact that the logical viability of induction does appear to rely on the validity of background knowledge which is *itself* inductively derived, is a genuine problem for anyone interested in the theoretical status of learning.

In this book we have sought to conceptualize learning in terms of the exploitation of regularity. We have also sought to get a better idea of what regularity is, using information theory (chapter 4) and a first-principles analysis of the way in which regularity can be broken down into logical categories (chapter 7). However, none of this really helps us much with respect to Hume. Nor does it eliminate the noted problem of circularity. But there are reasons for thinking that the extreme form of skepticism, exemplified by the Prosecution argument given above, overstates the case. To bring things into perspective, we need to go back to where we left off in chapter 4. We need, in particular, to investigate more fully the connection bewteen induction and *compression*.

9.7   Notes

1. Amusingly, Hume's law may be regarded as subject to itself.

2. In the wake of the '87 crash, the New York Stock Exchange took action to eliminate the risk of market meltdown. In particular, it created the "circuit breaker" mechanism in which trading is halted for one hour if the Dow Jones average falls more than 250 points in a day, and for two hours if it falls more than 400 points.

3. The word "induction" is derived from the Latin translation of Aristotle's *epagoge*.

4. This conclusion is actually false, since black swans exist in Australia.

5. From *Logic* III (viii).

6. Russell (1967).

7. The long-sustained failure of post-Humean philosophers to retrieve it from this plight has been dubbed the *scandal of philosophy*.

8. These arguments are based loosely on material in David Wolpert's no-free-lunch papers (Wolpert 1996a and 1996b) and Schaffer's related work (Schaffer 1994).

10

Phases of Compression

The First approached the Elephant
And, happening to fall
Against his broad and sturdy side,
At once began to bawl:
"God bless me, but the Elephant
Is very like a wall!"

The Second, feeling the tusk,
Cried, "Ho! what have we here
So very round and smooth and sharp?
To me 'tis very clear
This wonder of an Elephant
Is very like a spear!"

The Third approached the animal
And, happening to take
The squirming trunk within his hands,
Thus boldly up he spake:
"I see," quoth he, "The Elephant
Is very like a snake!"

John Godfrey Saxe[1]

10.1 Through a Double Slit Darkly

Experiment: Take a very small light source and place it on one side of an opaque surface. Make two small, parallel slits in the surface and place an opaque screen on its far side. Turn on the light source and observe the pattern thrown onto the screen by the separated light beams.

With a little luck, you will observe an unexpected phenomenon. The screen will be lit up with a pattern of parallel bands of light. These bands

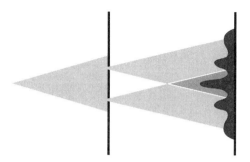

Figure 10.1
Double-slit effect

will be repeated for about a centimeter before they fade out and become too dim to see (see schematic diagram in figure 10.1).

This simple procedure involving surfaces and screens is, of course, the famous *double-slit* experiment, first performed by Thomas Young around 1800.[2] (Young actually used a third screen with a pinhole so as to minimize the size of the light source.) Rather obviously, the experiment produces a counterintuitive result. Instead of the uniform illumination of the screen that we expect, the procedure produces bands or "fringes" of light and dark. What could possibly account for this?

Thomas Young did not know what light was. But he reasoned that the bands had to be the result of interference between the separated light beams. He decided the light coming through the two slits must be behaving something like water, rippling outward in waves that would sometimes reinforce each other (in a process of "constructive interference") and sometimes cancel each other out (in a process of "destructive interference"). On this account, the explanation for the bands was straightforward. The lighter bands were caused by larger waves striking the screen. The darker bands were caused by smaller waves striking the screen. The general conclusion: light moves in waves, rather as water does.

Young's demonstration of the wave nature of light remained unquestioned for a hundred years. However, after 1900, the situation changed dramatically. Max Planck discovered that excited electrons emit and absorb energy only in specific amounts, which he termed *quanta*. Soon after, in 1905, Einstein theorized that energy itself is quantized. And using experimental work of Philipp Lenard, he demonstrated that light is made up of *particles* (photons). This work produced a deep crisis in physics. Scientists were faced with rock-solid demonstrations establishing (a) that light is made up of waves and (b) that light is made up of particles. How could these two apparently contradictory assertions possibly be reconciled?

Through the early years of the twentieth century, work by Louis de Broglie, Erwin Schrödinger, Werner Heisenberg, and others led to the emergence of *quantum mechanics* and the so-called *Copenhagen interpretation*, which attempted to explain the implications of quantum mechanics for physical reality. Central to the theory was the thesis that light was made neither of waves nor of particles but in fact had both a "wave nature" and a "particle nature," with the nature revealed in a specific instance being dependent on the experiment performed. The deeply unsettling implication of this was that physical reality could no longer be regarded as fully objective.

The pioneers of the new quantum mechanics struggled to make sense of this disconcerting result, with Heisenberg playing a leading role in the development of a new and revolutionary mind-set. His view was that the attempt to picture subatomic events led to confusion because the macroscopic, everyday concepts applied in the process had no meaning within the subatomic realm. He proposed instead a strictly mathematical approach that treated reality as consisting of just those properties which were measurable and any implications which could be mathematically derived from them. In his *Uncertainty Principle*, he gave the idea a compelling theoretical foundation. The principle established that we cannot measure both the position *and* the momentum of a particle. We can measure only one thing at a time, a fact implying that decisions made by the observer *necessarily* have an effect on the phenomenon observed. Therefore, no observation can be strictly objective. A subjective element is always present.

According to the Copenhagen interpretation of quantum mechanics, the world at the subatomic level is one in which there are no "hard" objects. We cannot talk about things existing or not existing. We can only talk about the *probability* of a particular type of measurement or test having a particular type of result. We have to accept, then, that the familiar world of solid objects bottoms out in a soupy blur in which probability is the only foundation. Newtonian variables such as position, trajectory, and momentum have to be viewed as "symptoms" that may or may not (be caused to) appear in certain situations.

A strange picture indeed; and to many physicists of the early twentieth century, worse than strange. It was, in fact, *unacceptable*. Einstein was famously unable to swallow the implications of quantum mechanics, reminding his collegues on a regular basis that "God does not play dice."[3] The assumption that physical reality must be describable in terms of macroscopic concepts (object, velocity, trajectory, etc.) was more or less an article of faith, as was the belief in the existence of objective reality. But intuition, as we have seen, can be very misleading. And the Newtonians of the "old physics" found themselves sailing in a kind of majestic but functionally deficient *Titanic*, directly into the ice field of quantum mechanics" unstoppable empirical success. The rest, as they say, is history.

10.2   Induction–Compression Duality

The temptation to try to understand natural processes in terms of concepts that make sense to us, that is, concepts which are useful to agents that must negotiate a particular physical universe—is naturally very strong. This book, it cannot be denied, has given in to the temptation to try to understand *learning* in such terms at every turn. But the story of the "new physics" is a powerful reminder that concepts of intuition may not be meaningful when applied outside their natural context. And we need to take account of this here, in our investigation of *induction*. There is no reason why the fundamental reality of this process should be comprehensible in terms of concepts that are useful and/or meaningful to us. There may be a deeper reality to the process that cannot be easily described in such terms. Just as it was with the new physics, so it may be that understanding induction (learning) requires the development of novel concepts which combine existing ideas in new ways.

In chapter 4 it was noted that the role of useful redundancy was to facilitate prediction, and that learning and data compression must therefore share the same goal—the goal of identifying useful redundancy. On this view, it is fairly obvious that the two processes are closely related. The only real difference seems to be the way the identified redundancy is utilized. In learning, redundancy is utilized for purposes (akin to) prediction. In data compression, it is utilized for purposes of cost minimization. Beyond that, the two appear to be near clones.

Is the situation with learning, then, comparable to the situation with light? Is it the case that what we are really confronted with is some underlying phenomenon that has both an "induction nature" and a "compression nature," with the nature being revealed in a specific case depending entirely on the question asked? And if this is the case, what are the practical implications? Will it pay us to reconceptualize our interest in terms of an induction/compression hybrid? Or does this disobey Occam's dictum (see below) disallowing the introduction of unnecessary entities? To answer these questions, we need a better understanding of what data compression is all about. We need to get a flavor of the techniques involved, the ways in which they are applied, and the measures and criteria by which success is evaluated. This is the goal of the next section.

10.3 Data Compression

The process of data compression, it turns out, is aptly named: it is literally the task of taking a body of data and compressing it into a smaller form. There are two main forms of the task: if the encoding is fully reversible (i.e., if the original data must be perfectly recoverable), then the process is *lossless*; otherwise, it is *lossy*. The degree of compression achieved in a given case is termed the *compression ratio*. This is defined as the ratio of the size of the original data to the size of the encoding. Thus if we have a data set that is 90 bytes long and we manage to compress it into an encoding of only 30 bytes, we have achieved a compression ratio of 3/1.

A simple technique for achieving lossless compression is *null suppression*. This involves replacing every sequence of nulls (spaces) with a special flag and a count of the number of nulls in the sequence. Naturally, the degree of compression that can be achieved by this move depends on the data involved. If null suppression is applied to data containing many lengthy sequences of nulls (e.g., records in which each field is padded out with nulls), then the savings will be considerable. If the method is applied to data with few null sequences (e.g., ASCII text), then the savings are likely to be far less significant.

There are several variations on the theme of sequence suppression. In *run-length encoding* we replace any sequence of identical characters with a flag, the character, and a count. In *bit mapping* we put several bytes together to form a bit map that states exactly where in the data the long sequences are located. In *half-byte packing* we encode one full byte in half a byte (four bits), and in *diatomic encoding* we squash two bytes into one.

10.4   Sequence Encoding and Ziv-Lempel Compression

A good coding scheme for a data set is clearly one that allows features appearing very frequently to be coded in a parsimonious way. Null suppression is a good coding scheme for data containing many sequences of nulls because it allows those sequences to be encoded using a single character. One way to generalize this is to say that a good code for a data set is one in which the length of a code for an arbitrary sequence is *inversely* related to the frequency of its occurrence. Shorter codes are to be associated with relatively frequent sequences. Longer codes should be associated with relatively infrequent sequences. Tightening this up a little, we may assert that the best code for a data set is one in which the lengths of codes are inversely *proportional* to the frequency of the corresponding encoded sequences.[4]

Unfortunately, although this definition makes perfect sense, it does not translate easily into a practical compression method. The problem is that in order to derive such a code for a given data set, frequencies for all possible sequences of data need to be identified in advance. The complexity or difficulty of this operation increases exponentially with the size of the data set. The strategy is thus impractical for realistic data sets. We can, of course, reduce the complexity of the problem by limiting the assumed length of sequences (in the limit, to a single character), but then we no longer have any guarantees that the coding system produced is the one we really want.

Although optimal codes (for sequences) cannot easily be derived on the fly, there are approximations of the approach that are effective in practice. The *Ziv-Lempel* compression methods, which form the basis of many modern compression packages, are relevant here. They operate in a rather cunning way. Rather than attempting to discover the optimal encoding scheme in advance, such methods simply read through the data, assigning a new code for each unique substring (sequence) encountered. Only substrings appearing in the data are assigned codes. The coding scheme thus produced is a rough approximation of an optimal code for sequences. But because the method efficiently exploits repetitions, the compression performance produced may be extremely good.

A compressor of this type—a Ziv-Lempel compressor—works as follows.[5] First, codes are assigned for all the *primitive substrings*, that is, all possible single characters. If the data consist of As and Bs, then this involves giving A the code 1 and B the code 2. Next the compressor reads through the data string. Each time it comes across a substring it has never seen before, it assigns that substring the next available code, that is, the next highest integer. It then outputs the code for the last substring it was looking at (which is the latest substring without its last character) and begins reading again from the current character.

Once the compression process is complete, all the string codes may be thrown away. Because of the way in which codes are generated, they can be automatically regenerated during decompression. The procedure is as follows. The compressor begins reading the compressed data, decoding them using the known codes for primitive strings. Each time the decompressor generates a new substring, it allocates a new code for it in the same way the compressor did. But because the codes generated by the compressor are generally at least one step behind the data, the decompressor finds that it usually knows the translation for a code *before* it first sees it.

There is, however, one situation in which the decompressor may come across a code for which it does not know the translation. If the original data string contains an overlapping repeat, such as the substring ABA in the string ABABA, then the compressor may immediately use the code it generated for the first instantiation in encoding the second. The decompressor is then "taken by surprise." It is confronted with a code for which it has not constructed a translation. However, from the facts that the code is known to have been newly minted, and to have been derived from an overlapping repeat, the decompressor can infer that the translation is the translation for the most recently seen code with its initial character tacked on the end.

Let us look at a concrete example of the Ziv-Lempel method in action. Assume we want to compress the data string ABCACAABABAC and that we know all the data are made up of A, B, and C characters. The compressor initializes its table to contain all the primitive strings, that is, A, B, and C. (The example is illustrated in figure 10.2.) It then begins to read through the original data string. After the first character has been read, the seen string is A. This already has the code 1, so the compressor continues. After the next character has been read, the seen string is AB. This has no code, so the code for A is outputted and the string AB is given the next code in sequence, 4. The string B already has a code, so the compressor continues. After the next character has been read, the seen string is BC. Again, this has no code, so the code for the previous seen string B is outputted and a new code (5) is created for BC. The seen string is now reinitialized to be C. Again, this string already has a code, so the compressor continues and reads CA. This has no code, so the compressor outputs the code for C and gives CA the next code (6). This process continues until the entire data string has been encoded.

The compressed representation is 1 2 3 1 6 4 9 3. In processing this, the decompressor must read through the codes, translating them and rebuilding the compressor's code table as it goes. The translations for the first four codes are all primitive strings and are thus readily translated into ABCA. Once this string has been derived, the decompressor can infer the translations for the compressor's first three codes: 4, 5, and 6. Thus, when the code 6 is read, the decompressor already has its translation to hand.

As noted, the decompressor *may* come across a code it does not already know, but only in the situation where the presence of an overlapping

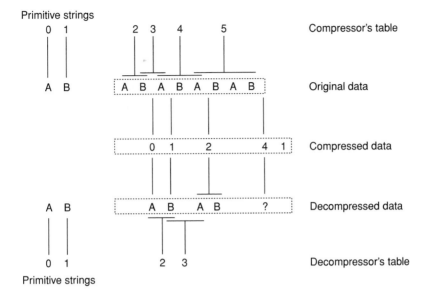

Figure 10.2
Illustration of Ziv-Lempel compression
The decompressor works one step behind the compressor and thus normally reconstructs each link in the string chain before its code is first seen. But if the original data string contains an overlapping repeat, as in ABABA, the compressor uses a code as soon as it has been generated (see code 9).

The decompressor now has to guess the translation for an unknown code. However, since the code is known to be (a) brand new (i.e., the last assigned code) and (b) derived from an overlapping repeat its translation must be the translation for the last seen code (4) with the initial character (A) tacked on the end.

repeat in the original data string has caused the compressor to assign a code and then *immediately* use it. In the example of figure 10.2, this happens in the case of code 9. However, the circumstances of this event mean that the decompressor can readily guess the correct translation.

10.5 Kolmogorov Complexity and the (Mythical) Perfect Compressor

The Ziv-Lempel method of compression aims to achieve *maximal* compression of a given body of data. Unfortunately, it does not achieve this goal. But let us consider for a moment what the implications might be if perfect compression could be achieved. The perfect compression method would take an arbitrary data set and eliminate *all* useful redundancy. If we were to calculate the difference between the size of the original data set and the size of the compressed encoding, we would then have a measure of the *total amount* of useful redundancy contained in the original data. By the same token, if we could measure the total amount of useful redundancy in any arbitrary data, we would then know how much compression *could* be achieved on that data set by a perfect compressor.

These ideas are at the heart of a body of theory known as Kolmogorov complexity theory,[6] which uses concepts of computation to make the idea of compression measurement more precise. The core of Kolmogorov complexity theory is the following assertion:

• The complexity of some data D is equal to the size of the smallest computer program that generates D.

Although this definition deals specifically in terms of computer programs, it is really just a restatement of the idea (already familiar from chapter 4) that the true complexity of some data set is equal to the size of its minimal encoding. Data sets that have smaller minimal encodings obviously can be generated by smaller computer programs. Data sets that have larger minimal encodings require larger computer programs. As an illustration of the idea, imagine that we have a body of data which lists all the multiplication tables from 1 to 10. We might suspect that the complexity of the data specifying such tables is lower than the complexity of, say, data specifying all British soccer match scores over the past ten years. The Kolmogorov complexity rule confirms the intuition. Multiplication tables can be generated from a summarizing formula or rule (i.e., a small computer program). Soccer scores—we hope—cannot. Thus the multiplication tables require a smaller generating program than the soccer data and are identified as having a lower Kolmogorov complexity.

At first sight, it may not be obvious why the central definition of Kolmogorov complexity theory deals in terms of generating computer programs. But the move turns out to be essential in order to achieve a coherent theory. If we attempt to operate purely in terms of minimal encodings—the compressed data—problematic ambiguities arise.

Imagine that we take an arbitrary data set and attempt to identify its smallest encoding *by hand*. To begin, we may try running different data-compression algorithms on the data set to see what encodings are produced and how big they are. But eventually it is going to hit home that if we place no constraints on the data-compression process being applied, there is nothing to stop us from constructing a special-purpose "compressor" that simply has the original data set stored inside it. Regardless of the size of the original data set, such a compressor could produce an "encoding" consisting of zero data!

Of course, the objection would then be raised that this algorithm is not a "proper" compression algorithm because it can possibly work for only a small number of data sets. But the Kolmogorov solution is neater and more general. The true size of an encoding, it declares, is to be measured in terms of the size of the encoding itself *plus* the size of the encoding *process*. This move automatically rules out special-purpose approaches since, on this basis, the size of any special-purpose encodings will turn out to be greater than the size of the original data. By stating that the real size of an encoding is to be defined in terms of the smallest generating computer program, Kolmogorov complexity theory neatly ensures that both the size of the encoding and that of the encoding process are taken into account.[7]

10.6 Randomness

Kolmogorov complexity theory has a range of interesting applications. But it is perhaps best known for what it has to say about *randomness*. Intuitively, we think of the concept of randomness as unambiguous and un-contentious. But the subject turns out to be a minefield. Programmers are used to the idea that computer systems implement *random number generators*, that is, functions which, when called, produce an apparently random number in some given range. Applying a random number generator (in the range 1–25) fifteen times, we might obtain the following numbers:

19 7 8 18 8 18 13 14 19 17 0 13 3 14 12

Do these numbers really form a random selection? Visual inspection reveals no obvious pattern. And it is likely that they would pass most statistical tests of randomness. The numbers appear to be a formless collection of random choices. But, of course, since computers cannot really do anything without a reason, we know that the numbers cannot really have been selected by chance. They must have been selected using an algorithm designed to give the *appearance* of randomness.

Essentially, random-number-generator (*RNG*) algorithms operate by attempting to generate each number (in the specified range) equally often but not in any particular pattern or sequence. All too often, however, the underlying algorithm "shows through" and the randomness is revealed for the fake it really is.[8] This is why computer-implemented RNGs are termed *pseudo-random number generators*. To achieve genuine randomness, it would seem to be necessary to derive the numbers from genuinely random events in the real world. But outside of the nondeterministic world of quantum physics, these are hard to come by.[9] The implementation of randomness is thus a serious practical problem.

Kolmogorov complexity theory makes a key contribution here because it offers us a straightforward way of defining what randomness really is. Note that any data set D can always be generated by a computer program that simply *prints* D. The smallest program that generates D cannot be any bigger than D itself. The size of D is thus an upper bound on the Kolmogorov complexity of D. From this observation we derive a neat definition. Since completely random data are, by definition, totally lacking in any sort of regularity, we know that any sort of compression must be ruled out. Thus the minimal encoding (or generating computer program) for a completely random data set must have the maximum size, which means it must be as big as the original data set itself. The Kolmogorov complexity of a completely random data set is therefore necessarily equal to the size of the data set itself. Any data set D whose Kolmogorov complexity is equal to the size of D is thus determined to be completely random!

10.7   Minimum Description Length

Since our interest in data compression (and Kolmogorov theory) arises from our interest in learning (induction), we clearly want to know more about the relationship between the two processes. To come to grips with this, we need to delve a little more deeply into the literature. Compression/induction linkages crop up with high frequency throughout the computationally oriented fields of learning research.[10] A common theme is the idea that data compression may form a "guidance system" for learning. Roughly speaking, the proposal is this: by attending to the degree to which learning (implicitly or explicitly) compresses the input data, a learning method can measure its *progress*—it can test the degree to which it is exploiting useful redundancy. By making progress toward the goal of maximum compression, the learner then automatically moves in the direction of optimal prediction and generalization.

Of course, for the idea to work in practice, it is essential for the learner to be given a way of measuring the "degree of compression" achieved by a given act of learning. A promising approach here is the *minimum description length (MDL)* framework of Rissanen.[11] This provides a framework in which the learner can measure achieved compression, factoring in the associated cost of the encoding/decoding process.

Approaches such as MDL have considerable conceptual appeal. And for present purposes they represent a logical end point in the attempt to blur the distinction between induction and compression. But whether MDL offers a *practical* advantage is not so clear. Compressive efficacy is, as we have seen, the direct analogue of predictive efficacy. Thus one has to assume that methods which will work well within the MDL paradigm will be *exactly* those methods which work well outside of it. The pursuit of predictive efficacy is logically equivalent to the pursuit of better compression. Thus we cannot harbor any great hope of improving performance simply by substituting one perspective for the other.

More interesting for present purposes is the question of the status of data-compression methods with respect to the classification schemes we have used for learning. The key issue for learning methods, we saw in chapter 7, is whether they fall within the finitely complex nonrelational camp or the infinitely complex relational camp. Logically speaking, compression methods face the same dichotomy. And we naturally expect there to be a reasonable spread of methods across the two categories. But, surprisingly, this is not what we find in practice. All compression methods fall unambiguously into the *nonrelational* camp. Compression methods adopting a specifically relational approach are notable by their absence. The situation with respect to methods such as Ziv-Lempel coding, Huffman coding, and null suppression is particularly clear. All these methods seek to exploit the presence of repetitions in the data. Repetitions represent similarity in its perfect form. All such methods thus pursue the nonrelational, similarity-oriented strategy.

Several factors may account for the lack of relational compression methods. First there is the general difficulty of relational processing to consider. Then there is its inevitable lack of generality (both issues discussed in chapter 8). But beyond these built-in drawbacks, there is something more fundamental to consider. Data compression methods take a data set and encode it in a more compact form. This process can be viewed as involving the application of encoding functions to the original data. Nonrelational data compression involves the application of nonrelational encoding functions, and relational data compression involves the application of relational encoding functions. And here, we begin to see the source of the difficulty.

A relational function necessarily computes a relational property of its input values. This cannot unambiguously identify the original input values, on pain of undermining the function's relational classification. Were it to do so, the function would be fully reversible and thus more properly viewed in terms of a 1-to-1 labeling. In the application of a relational function, then, there is an accompanying and arguably necessary loss of information. Relational methods cannot achieve lossless compression due to definitional limitations.

Relational data compression, then, has to be written off as a nonstarter. But what of induction's other cousin, decryption? Is it meaningful to talk about relational and nonrelational decryption processes? If so, what real-world processes would they correspond to? The situation here is practically identical to the one associated with relational data compression. Effective decryption *necessitates* reversibility. But the definitional irreversibility of relational encoding/encryption functions implies that "relational encryption" could never be a useful methodology.

10.8 Compression Phases

There is some disappointment, perhaps, in the realization that the induction/compression connection is of limited practical value. But the connection remains significant for the way in which it stimulates ideas. In taking account of the relationship between induction and compression, we begin to get a better view of learning's hidden dimensions. We begin to see how learning forms one element in a system of processes, all of which perform some sort of data- or information-mutation process.

Induction (learning) is the case with which we are most familiar. Its role is to take raw data and extract or "purify" the embodied information. Data compression performs a similar operation, but with the aim of minimizing the size of the produced encoding. Induction performed cooperatively and in a controlled manner is the process we call science, a principal subtask of which is *explanation*. Here the aim is to take raw data and construct a conceptual framework that renders raw data comprehensible, the goal of compactness being downgraded while meaningfulness and interpretability become central.

Two further variations are encryption and prediction. Encryption, the process discussed in chapter 6, is something of an oddity. Here the aim is to *generate* raw data from information and to do it in such a way as to maximally hinder any processes that attempt to reverse the process. Prediction is also a data-generation procedure, but here there is no attempt to hinder reversal. The aim is simply to flesh out an already redundant encoding of the original information.

One way to visualize the relationship between these processes is shown in figure 10.3. I call this diagram "Phases of Compression." It comprises a two-dimensional space in which each axis measures a particular property of an informational process. The vertical axis measures the degree to which the process is involved in "expansion," that is, the generation of data. The horizontal axis measures the degree to which the process is engaged in information simplification.

Superimposed on these axes is an elliptical orbit. The various informational processes are portrayed as planets orbiting along the ellipse. An important feature of the diagram is the upper left quadrant, which is a no-go area for all processes. No "planets" exist in this quadrant because simplification cannot be achieved through data expansion (or vice versa). I call it the *Occam quadrant* on the grounds that it is the part of the space in which processes would necessarily confront (or generate) gratuitous entities, in direct contradiction to Occam's Razor (see next section).

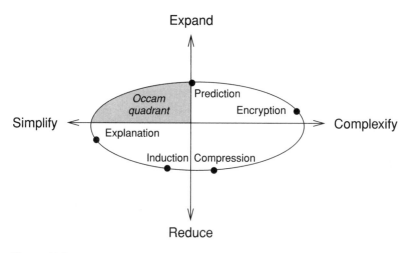

Figure 10.3
The phases of compression

This scheme is just one of many possible visualizations and may well not be the best approach. But it does at least have the virtue of automatically reminding us of its own inherent artifice. Looking at an elliptical orbit puts us in mind of Kepler's work on Mars and the discovery of the first law of planetary motion. Popping into consciousness there should then be a recollection of the way Kepler's laws were eventually shown to be only *approximately* correct—to be special cases of situations that were better handled by relativity theory. The net effect should then be a powerful reminder of Hume's rule asserting the potential fallibility of *all* theoretical constructs—even the ones optimistically elevated to the status of laws.

10.9   Hume Slashed by Occam's Razor

Treating induction as a variation on the theme of compression reveals an interesting paradox. When we look at learning-related processes, we quickly encounter Hume's problem: the observation that any guess is always fundamentally uncertain, and complete success in an inductive process is thus impossible to achieve. But when we turn attention to compression-related processes, Hume's problem seems to evaporate into thin air. With a compression process, success seems rather *straightfor-wardly* achieved. Data compression is accomplished just in case the relevant source data set is reduced in size. Why is there such a difference between the two scenarios? Why, in particular, does there appear to be no equivalent of Hume's problem in the realm of data compression?

To dissolve the paradox, we need to go back and briefly consider the works of the fourteenth-century English philosopher William of Occam. Occam is remembered for his use of the *principle of parsimony*, which states, "It is vain to do with more what can be done with less." According to this rule, explanations should not be any more complex than is necessary. Explanatory entities should not be multiplied beyond necessity, and pseudo-explanatory entities should be ruthlessly eliminated. More than six centuries after Occam's death, scientists continue to treat this rule as a key principle of scientific work, and the process of simplifying a theory is often described as the application of *Occam's Razor*. However, despite the longevity of the principle, it is generally believed to have *no* underlying proof or logical derivation. Rather, it is viewed as a rule of thumb or a heuristic.

For present purposes the Razor is, of course, significant for the way in which it underlines the symmetry between data compression and induction. It effectively states that explanations are improved by *compression*, thus covertly revealing that the goal of induction-related processes is equivalent to the goal of compression-related processes. But the Razor also helps us to resolve the paradox of the "missing Hume problem."

Occam's Razor deals with the process of explanation, which, as we have seen, is a type of induction. But whereas induction is associated with worries about the *certainty* of conclusions (predictions), Occam's Razor puts the spotlight on a different sort of success. It emphasizes the *improvement* of theories rather than the certainty of their conclusions. In a sense, Occam's Razor invites us to forget that explanation is a type of induction and to regard it instead as a type of compression. Once this move has been made, it becomes natural to treat success as relative rather than absolute. Hume's problem, which is associated exclusively with the problem of absolute certainty, then disappears.

Occam's Razor is thus a way of cashing in the noted induction/compression duality so as to eliminate the problem of induction. Hume's problem, we know, cannot be solved *as is*. However, using the Razor, we render it virtually irrelevant for all purposes except the slightly unrealistic task of deriving 100% guaranteed-correct predictions. On this view, the whole notion of a "missing problem" falls away. Hume's thesis is associated exclusively with (the idea of) an *optimally* successful data-mutation process. There is no Hume's problem in data compression simply because optimal data compression is irrelevant in practice and known to be impossible in principle.

Occam's Razor effectively imports the relativistic success criterion of the data compression scenario into the inductive realm. But, despite suspicions, there is no reason to think that this transplantation undermines the validity of the criterion. Scientific explanation, we have noted, is a key member of the induction/compression family. As such, its role may be understood in terms of the improvement of predictive accuracy. The operational significance of simplicity—the quality relevant to the Razor—then comes into focus. Simpler inductive inferences necessarily make fewer assumptions about the data. Every assumption has an even chance of being invalid. Thus simpler inductive inferences will, in general, be predictively more successful. If it has any effect at all, then, the application of Occam's Razor within any sort of inductive process *must* improve predictive accuracy. Far from being a rule of thumb, Occams' Razor might thus be viewed as a near tautology. Scientists have been doing the right thing all along, and for reasons that the theory of induction/compression duality suggests are *demonstrably* correct.

10.10   Notes

1. This is an extract from Saxe's "Parable of the Blind Men and the Elephant."

2. Various animations showing the effect are currently available via the Internet page numerix.us.es/numex.html.

3. Writing in the London *Observer* on April 5, 1964, for example, Einstein said, "I cannot believe that God plays dice with the Cosmos."

4. A code that satisfies this criterion is known, technically, as a *statistical code*. Character-based codes of this type, *Huffman codes*, are known to be mathematically optimal in certain situations.

5. This specification is based loosely on Terry Welch's LZW compression scheme, currently described at http://www.ifi.uio.no/in383/introduction.shtml.

6. The theory, also known as *algorithmic information theory*, was developed independently by Andrei Kolmogorov, Gregory Chaitin, and Ray Solomonoff.

7. The MDL framework achieves the same effect by compelling final costs to be calculated in terms of the encoding and the encoding process.

8. In fact the numbers in the "random" sequence above are the alphabetical character positions for the string "thisisnotrandom."

9. Consider the process of tossing a coin—perhaps the most common way of obtaining a "random" decision. When a coin is tossed into the air, we assume that it will land a particular way up by *chance*. But this is not really the case. The coin will land a particular side up due to the way it is flipped, the direction and velocity of the wind, the weight of the coin, the slipperiness of the fingers, and so on. The outcome is not really the result of chance. But it is due to such a complicated web of hard-to-test properties that no human being can easily *predict* the final outcome. For all intents and purposes the outcome is random.

10. My doctoral thesis, "Concept Learning as Data Compression" (Thornton 1989), provides some pointers.

11. Rissanen (1987).

11

Protorepresentational Learning

Actually, I know that.
I already thought it in my head.
If I don't know something then I just make it up in my head.
There's a tool thing in my brain—all lots of tool.
And in my brain I had little things I don't know,
and they are the things I don't know.
So I just make it up in my brain.
Then I know them all of my life.

James Thornton (age 3)

11.1   The Cincinnati Story

Many will have heard the sad story of the Cincinnati System. In the mid-1990s, a consortium of prestigious U.S. institutions began a collaborative effort with the aim of developing a world-beating computer poker player. According to the consortium's 40-page manifesto, development of the system would take up to two years; the final product would be entered into the All-American Poker Championships (the AAPC). Machine-learning technologies would be exploited to avoid the necessity for complex programming. The system would be exposed to an extremely large number of expert-level poker games. It would then be trained to produce a corresponding level of performance.

Development of the system, code-named Cincinnati after the Steve McQueen movie *The Cincinnati Kid*, proceeded smoothly. However, when the time came to enter the system in the 1998 AAPC, things began to go embarrassingly wrong. The consortium's plan was to eliminate the possibility of system failure by utilizing a belt-and-suspenders approach.

Cincinnati was configured to use not one but *four* different machine-learning modules, each based on a state-of-the-art methodology: back-propagation, C4.5, LVQ, and RBF. To achieve reasonable real-time performance, the consortium had also constructed special-purpose hardware modules for computationally intensive procedures such as k-NN.

Mindful of the publicity implications, the organizers of the AAPC had promised full cooperation with the consortium's challenge. But relations between the two bodies quickly deteriorated. Before the first game was played, a crisis developed when it was discovered that the doors to the main arena were not wide enough to accommodate the articulated truck carrying the consortium's backpropagation module. As a result the module had to be installed *outside* the arena and extensive wiring had to be laid down in order to establish connections with the system's table-side setup.

This was just the beginning. During its first game, Cincinnati played very badly, betting large amounts of money on the basis of low-ranking hands while throwing away hands of higher rank. The system also malfunctioned repeatedly, requiring lengthy remedial attention on each occasion. In the latter part of the game, players found themselves forced to wait for up to an hour for Cincinnati to lay a bet. One by one the players resigned their hands and left the table, eventually allowing Cincinnati to win by default.

Had Cincinnati managed to remain in the competition for any length of time, the AAPC organizers would undoubtedly have had to take some sort of action, the obvious remedy being the introduction of a time limit for betting decisions. However, in the event no action was necessary. The system was conclusively knocked out in the second round, allowing the competition to continue to its natural conclusion without further upset.

The day after Cincinnati's humiliating defeat, the consortium of developers held an informal postmortem. What had gone wrong? How was it possible, after the expenditure of so many thousands of dollars, that the machine had been wiped out of the competition before even making it through the warm-up rounds? Discussions were heated and sometimes acrimonious. Accusations and counteraccusations flew. Finally it emerged that some of the key testing procedures had not been carried out in the *usual* manner. The contingent responsible for this aspect of the work accidentally revealed that they had not bothered to "formally" test the results of the training procedures they had applied. This would have been enormously time-consuming, they argued, and would not have provided any useful information. The methodologies utilized were tried-and-tested, state-of-the-art techniques. It was beyond "reasonable doubt" that they would generate the expected levels of performance.

Unhappily for those concerned, the debacle of Cincinnati's AAPC performance showed otherwise. But the problem, it eventually transpired, had absolutely nothing to do with the learning algorithms used. It had nothing to do with the configuration or positioning of the hardware modules. And it had nothing to do with the complex multiplexing subsystem, or with the user interface. Rather, it had to do with *the data*. The system had been designed to use a simple card-based input language, which enabled poker situations to be presented in terms of collections of card values. Each input value in a Cincinnati training pair thus represented the face value of a *single* card, while output values specified appropriate actions for the relevant hand.

Using a card-based data language for a card-based problem *seems* reasonable enough. But it is actually a quite risky approach. In poker, as in most card games, the key entities are complete hands—full houses, runs, straights, flushes, and so on. These are defined in terms of *relationships* among cards. They are typically not defined in terms of absolute card values. To be an effective poker player, it is essential to be able to operate in terms of these relational entities. Ditto for the poker learner.

Cincinnati's card-based input language effectively guaranteed a worst-case scenario for the learning modules. It ensured that nonrelational learning processes could do *nothing other* than exploit effects involving nonrelational situations, such as games won on the basis of high-value cards. This might not have been a problem had the consortium realized the consequences of their data design and opted to utilize suitable relational methods. But, unfortunately, their approach focused exclusively on "state-of-the-art" *nonrelational* methods. The consortium thus ruined its chances in its very first design decision. Nothing that it subsequently did in terms of adding hardware, improving functionality, increasing speeds, or enhancing integration could make the slightest difference. Cincinnati was a white elephant among white elephants: an enormously powerful poker-learning machine capable of learning almost *none* of the salient facts about poker.

11.2   Relational Learning Revisited

The Cincinnati story reminds us that researchers ignore the problem of relational learning at their peril. But finding a good solution to the problem may be surprisingly difficult. Chapter 8 showed how the level of performance attainable on relational problems using supercharged fence-and-fill methods is inevitably limited. It also showed that while ideal levels of performance can be obtained from pick-and-mix methods, these require a ready supply of appropriate background knowledge—all too often a resource that is simply not available. The machine-learning practitioner thus faces a dilemma in selecting a suitable strategy for the relational domain.

It is sometimes claimed that the modest levels of performance obtainable from supercharged fence-and-fill methods on relational problems are generally sufficient for practical purposes. According to this satisficing theory, learning of the pick-and-mix variety is never required in practice. Therefore its intrinsic difficulties are largely irrelevant to the practitioner.

The argument seems a little hard to swallow, given the way it discounts the importance of accurate prediction. But we should not leap to conclusions: there is another argument that achieves more or less the same effect in a less dubious manner. This proposes that *evolution* can be relied upon to take the strain. The need for accurate generalization may indeed entail effective relational learning, it concedes, and this may *indeed* presume the availability of suitable domain knowledge. But we should not think of this as a problem. Evolution can be relied upon to create whatever "background knowledge" is required, when and where necessary. Or so the story goes.

Unfortunately, while both of these arguments are seductive, neither is completely coherent. Even allowing that accurate generalization may not be a necessity in all practical scenarios, there are still profound difficulties in the idea that supercharged fence-and-fill methods can independently satisfy all requirements. Learning, in any natural context, has the appearance of being a *constructive* operation. The learning of one thing tends to open up the possibility of the learning of another, which itself may facilitate further learning events. The implication is that natural forms of learning are able to treat the *products* of any particular learning event as *inputs* into another. Exactly how this is best implemented remains an open question. But what is clear is that the fence-and-fill method of capturing relational properties in terms of their nonrelational side effects, probably will *not* be an effective approach. If learning is to build constructively on the identification of certain relationships, then those relationships presumably need to be explicitly identified. Implicit tagging in terms of accidental, statistical accompaniments looks to be inadequate.

But even as we reject the satisficing, pro–fence-and-fill argument, we see that there are still more profound difficulties with the alternative "evolutionary" stance. Invoking evolution as a kind of benevolent uncle who provides requisite background knowledge on demand simply relocates the problem of acquisition out of the learning context and into the evolutionary one. The best we can achieve here is the chance to reconceptualize our enterprise as an investigation of the properties of evolution rather than of learning. And appealing as this may seem, it is worth remembering that for many years there has been a fruitful exchange of ideas between learning and evolutionary research fields. Thus the simple act of moving from one paradigm to the other is unlikely to turn up any novel solutions.

The problem of relational learning, then, remains open. And here, in this penultimate chapter of the book, a plausible although still largely untested solution will be sketched out. This is the *truth-from-trash (TFT)* model of learning, which utilizes fence-and-fill learning but in the form of a *subroutine* rather than as a core operation.

11.3   Truth from Trash

To understand what the truth-from-trash method is all about, we need to go back to the origins of the problem it tries to solve. In particular we need to focus attention on the character of relational training data. Consider, for example, the training set shown in figure 11.1. These are training data for a relational problem that will feature later on in the

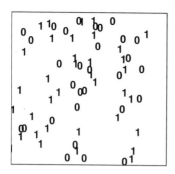

Figure 11.1
Relational training set

chapter. The data points give the appearance of being very disorganized: it would seem to be difficult, if not impossible, to separate them using any simple partitioning scheme.

However, when we scrutinize the data carefully, the initial impression of a disordered, random distribution of data points begins to recede. It is not that there are *no* clusters to be discerned. It is just that the clusters present are small and indistinct—surrounded on all sides by differently labeled data points. As we saw in chapters 7 and 8, this type of local order can sometimes be exploited for purposes of generalization. But, as we have just noted, both of the conventional approaches create problematic resourcing difficulties. Using the (supercharged) fence-and-fill approach, we are faced with an insatiable appetite for bounding constructs. Using the pick-and-mix approach, we are faced with a fundamental addiction to background knowledge.

The truth-from-trash model attempts to get beyond this face-off. It involves the application of a standard fence-and-fill operation in a recursive fashion, with the boundaries generated in each cycle being utilized *constructively* in the formation of a compositional partitioning scheme.

Let us see what this means in practice, when we try to process a real body of data. Utilizing a TFT approach, we would proceed as follows. In the first step, we apply a conventional fence-and-fill operation to derive an initial partitioning of the data. On the assumption that the problem is relational, the data are highly disordered and the initial partitioning is not useful in itself. And rather than using it for purposes of generating predictions directly, we use it as the basis for a recoding operation. The effect of this is to increase, to some extent, the degree of order in the data —to draw data points with the same label closer together. With the new encoding of the data to hand, we then proceed to apply the entire process recursively. To achieve this, we apply the fence-and-fill method to the *recoded* data and then reapply the recoding step.

Each time around the loop, we generate a new recoding of the data. In spatial terms, the effect is to gradually "push" identically labeled data points closer together. The result is that the performance of our basic fence-and-fill method *improves* over time. Eventually a point is reached when the application of the fence-and-fill method produces satisfactory predictive performance. At this point, we terminate the learning process.

A convenient way to summarize the TFT process is as a recursive procedure of three distinct steps. Written out in pseudocode, they are as follows.

1. Use the chosen fence-and-fill method to process the current input data, that is, to find regions of uniformly labeled stimuli.
2. Recode the current input data so as to draw identically labeled data points closer together. (As noted, the nature of the recoding step is not fixed. Any recoding operation may be used, provided it has the prescribed effect; that is, provided it has the effect of increasing global organization.)
3. Assign the derived data to be the current data and apply the procedure recursively until data are generated that can be satisfactorily processed solely by the fence-and-fill method.

The end product of this cyclical process is a sequence of recodings of the original data, each of which exhibits an increased level of global organization—that is, more pronounced clustering. Within the process, uniformly labeled data points "gravitate" toward each other. Each cycle thus sees a little more organization being extracted from the statistical "trash" that remains.

The number of recodings that will need to be derived in a particular case depends on the problem, of course, but also on the complexity and sophistication of the recoding step. With a more sophisticated recoding operation, we can expect a greater enhancement of global organization to be achieved at each step. But we then pay a price in terms of operating costs. With a less sophisticated operation, we expect more recoding steps to be required but that each one will cost us less. There is thus a depth versus width trade-off. A sophisticated recoding step means that only a shallow hierarchy of recodings will be required. But the recoding operation itself is more complex, giving us a result that is "short and fat." With a more primitive recoding step, a larger hierarchy of recodings will be required but the recoding step is simple, giving us a result that is "long and thin."

11.4   Why TFT Is Not Just Supercharged Fence-and-Fill

At first sight, the truth-from-trash procedure seems to resemble the typical supercharged fence-and-fill methodology of chapter 8. The idea seems to be to take an ordinary fence-and-fill method and provide it with the means of piling up a superposition of partitions. But TFT learning differs from supercharged fence-and-fill learning in an important way. Recall that the essence of supercharging is the utilization of a large number of simple partitions. But, crucially, these are utilized as *independent* entities. The aim is thus essentially the same as that of the standard fence-and-fill method—to discover some set of simple partitions that will adequately discriminate differently instantiated regions of the input space. The supercharged fence-and-fill method remains committed to the assumption of input-space clustering. The only real difference is that it can bring more bounding resources to bear and thus obtain a more graceful degradation in performance.

Unfortunately, as has been noted, in the relational scenario, we do not expect to see *meaningful* input-space clustering. In such scenarios, the supercharged fence-and-fill method is trying to manufacture a silk purse out of a sow's ear and progress can be achieved only at the price of profligate resource commitment. In the truth-from-trash method, by contrast, learning is undertaken constructively. By interleaving a recoding step between each layer of the constructed hierarchy, the method divorces itself from any assumption of cluster *meaningfulness*. Although TFT assumes there will be *some* local order (at each level of the hierarchy), it does not assume that this will be meaningfully related to the underlying problem. It simply assumes that it will be useful for deriving the next recoding.

Instead of spending resources to obtain a sufficiently large number of simple partitions (and paying a price in terms of lost generalization), the TFT method exploits the synergy between a simple partitioning operation and a simple recoding operation. By constructing a hierarchy of interleaved boundaries and recodings, it provides itself with the machinery for picking out arbitrary selections of data points. It thus produces and appropriately customizes the nongeometric partitions that are the required result of relational learning.

11.5   From Virtual Sensors to Symbol Processing

The TFT procedure is a relational-learning procedure and, like any other relational-learning algorithm, its aim is to identify the relationship that underlies the input data. But it goes about this task in an unconventional way. It does not produce a symbolic representation of the relationship or anything similar. Rather, it produces a (final) recoding space that encapsulates the relationship *implicitly*. Data points within the space are organized so as to reflect the degree to which they exhibit the relevant relationship. This means we can treat the dimensions of such a space as *measuring* the relationship. Another way to view the TFT process is, thus, as a means of creating *virtual sensors* for relevant relationships. The TFT method can then be said to produce truth from trash in the sense that it incrementally establishes access to "true" relational properties of the learner's sensory environment.

Where learning is constructive—that is, where the learner reuses the results of one learning operation as inputs in another—we can justifiably say that such virtual sensors are utilized by the agent[1] as data sources. In this case, the signals generated by the virtual sensors have a *representational* status because they are effectively used by the agent as symbols. Learning agents that engage in virtual-sensor usage of this form thus engage in a primitive form of *symbol processing*. (This idea will be further explored below.)

11.6   SCIL Learning—a Simple TFT Approach

Any method that implements the three-step procedure described above can be deemed a valid truth-from-trash method. But there are many possible implementations. Every pairing between a valid fence-and-fill learning method and a plausible recoding strategy provides a unique TFT method. Here, I will describe one very simple approach that I call the split-centers-in-layers (SCIL) method. The core of the algorithm is the center-splitting operation from chapter 6. This LVQ/ID3 hybrid generates a representation in terms of centers. Prediction and classification are then effected, using the "nearest-center" rule.

SCIL learning combines the center-splitting method with a simple recoding operation. In this, the current data points are ordered according to their associated output. (This assumes there is a defined ordering of outputs, for instance, that outputs are represented numerically.) The algorithm generates *derived* data based on two variables, referred to as the x and y coordinates below. The x coordinate of each derived data point is the linear position within the ordering of the original data point's nearest exemplar (which may be the data point itself), and the y coordinate is the proximity of the original data point to its nearest exemplar.

This recoding step sets the x coordinate of recoded data points according to the output label of its nearest exemplar. If we are dealing with Boolean data (positive and negative data points), the general effect is to move to the right all data points that are close to positive exemplars, and to the left all datapoints that are close to negative exemplars. Depending on the current level of clustering, this will create a degree of improvement in the global organization of the data points; that is, it will tend to push *all* negative data points to the left and *all* positive data points to the right.

In addition, there is the effect of the y coordinate to consider. As noted, the y coordinate of each new point is derived from the proximity of the (corresponding) original data point to its nearest exemplar. If there is even a modest degree of clustering, then we will expect to see identically labeled data points closer to their nearest exemplars than nonidentically labeled data points. Thus identically labeled data points will have higher y coordinates than nonidentically labeled data points. In columns associated with a positive exemplar, we should then see positive data points at the top and negative data points at the bottom, and vice versa for columns associated with a negative exemplar.

With Boolean (binary) labeled data points, the general effect of this recoding strategy is to push the data points toward a "flag" configuration with positive data points in the top left and bottom right corners and negative data points in the bottom left and top right corners. This configuration represents one of the simplest forms of clustering and thus is readily exploited by any fence-and-fill method. Of course, the amount of progress made in each cycle depends on the original degree of clustering. In general, all we can expect is that the orderliness of the data will be enhanced in each cycle. The achievement of a perfect configuration can be expected to involve several phases of processing.

11.7   SCIL Learning in the Warehouse Domain

To illustrate the way the SCIL method works in practice, we will revisit the warehouse domain, previously featured in chapters 2, 5, and 8. Let us imagine that following its successful utilization of a "robotic security guard," the warehousing company decides to push its utilization of robots one stage further. Word is passed down that the company bosses wish to utilize suitably programmed forklifts in the key task of *truck loading*.

This task involves moving objects from the warehouse area through the doors into a loading area, an operation that turns out to be less straightforward than it seems. When a truck becomes available, objects needing to be loaded must be moved in the right sequence—larger objects going first and smaller objects following. To complicate the situation, trucks become available on an irregular and unpredictable basis. Thus particular movements of objects cannot be scheduled for particular times. They have to be decided on a dynamic basis.

Once again, the company decides to exploit the possibilities of machine learning. First, it installs a traffic-light system above the warehouse doors. This display has three lights, colored red, green, and orange. The forklifts are then equipped with light sensors and programmed so that activation of the orange light causes them to attempt to transport a randomly selected object to the loading area. Activation of the green light causes the forklift to proceed through the doors. Activation of the red light causes the forklift to return the object to the shelf.

Following the installation of a couple of heat sensors (borrowed from a redundant alarm system) in suitable locations above the doors and the loading area, a human loading expert is utilized to handcraft a large set of training examples. Each input is to be a combination of sensor signals corresponding to a particular doorway. With each of these, the expert associates an appropriate traffic-light signal—1 representing activation of the green light, 0 representing activation of the red light. The plan is then to apply a machine-learning technique to the training set so as to derive a system for semiautomatic control of the traffic lights (and thus semi-automatic control of the truck-loading process).

Suffice it to say that the problem at hand is characteristically relational with respect to the input variables used. The generation of appropriate traffic-light signals depends critically on the relationship between the size of the object being transported (indicated by the door-area sensor) and the current state of loading of the current truck (indicated by the loading-area sensor). Output signals therefore depend on a relational property of the input signals. The net effect, as expected, is that the training data show little discernible clustering. The training data generated are in fact the disorganized data in figure 11.1.

Application of the center-splitting method to the training data generates 12 centers in the configuration shown in figure 11.2. Each center is enclosed by an inner and an outer sphere. Data points within inner spheres are correctly classified (by the nearest-center rule) using the relevant center. Data points within outer spheres have the relevant center as

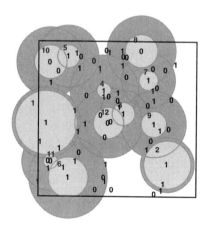

Figure 11.2
Generalization performance

their nearest center but are not necessarily correctly classified. The generalization performance of the method (at this level) can thus be determined by deriving the proportion of data points that do not share a class label with their nearest center.

Following the same conventions, figure 11.3 illustrates the entire processing cycle of the SCIL method applied to this data set. This version of the diagram is somewhat more complex. Instead of a single rectangle representing the original sensory space, we now have three rectangles representing the original space and two internal spaces derived during processing. The top right rectangle represents the first derived space and the bottom left rectangle represents the second derived space. Note how the general effect of the recodings is to "push" positive data points (1's) up

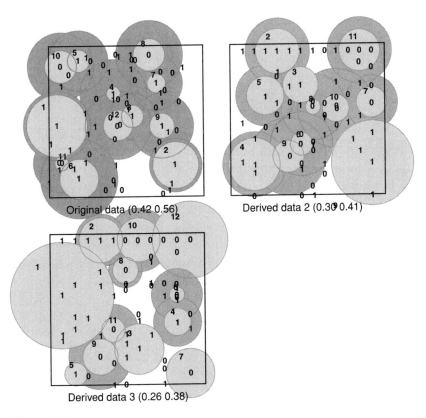

Original data (0.42 0.56)

Derived data 2 (0.30 0.41)

Derived data 3 (0.26 0.38)

Figure 11.3
Processing cycle of the SCIL method

and to the left, and the negative data points (0's) down and to the right. In the second derived space, we have a relatively good separation between the two groups. The application of the center-splitting method thus identifies some large and well-populated clusters. The generalization performance obtained is considered satisfactory, and processing terminates.

As was noted, in a "recoding cascade" generated by TFT learning, the dimensions of the final recoding space will typically measure or detect the relational property or properties underlying the mapping. In this particular example, the effect is rather pronounced—as it was designed to be. The original mapping was based on a relational effect between two abstract variables, the size of the object currently being transported to the loading bay and the timing of the movement within the current wagon-loading process. The recoding process used in SCIL forces the derivation of two-dimensional representations of the data, which in this case is exactly what is required. Thus the dimensions of the final recoding space in this example are expected to approximately measure the hidden variables upon which the original relational effect was based, namely, object size and movement timing.

In fact, when we examine the organization of the data points, this is *exactly* the effect that is discovered. Movements involving relatively large objects correspond to data points occupying the lower half of the final space. Movements that occur toward the later part of a particular wagon-loading operation correspond to data points occupying the left half of the final space. This space thus forms what is, in some sense, a reconceptualization of the sensed environment, rendered in terms of those abstract variables which are salient for the task, "loading time" and "object size." In some sense, the TFT learning in this example invents these notions and then utilizes them to simplify the task.

11.8   Representational Implications

We have seen that when relational learning is attempted using a supercharged fence-and-fill method, compromise is the inevitable result. Such methods share the bias of the basic fence-and-fill methodology—they operate in the hope of exploiting meaningful input-space clustering. But since no such clustering exists in the (nondegenerate) relational scenario, there is no hope of truly satisfactory levels of performance.

In the truth-from-trash model, the assumption of meaningful input-space clustering is eliminated. The basic partitioning methodology of the fence-and-fill process is retained but is now augmented by the provision of the constructive recoding operation. The result is that the fence-and-fill method no longer carries full responsibility for finding a solution. Instead it becomes a "cog in the works." Its role is to provide the means of exploiting useful nonrelational effects in a constructive collaboration with the chosen recoding operation.

As we have seen, the result of a successful TFT application to a relational problem is a hierarchy of recodings of the relevant sensory data. The dimensions of the top-level space in this hierarchy effectively measure or test the underlying relationship(s). And the sequence of partitionings and recodings that underlies the construction of data points in this space can thus be viewed as implementing virtual sensors for implicit, relational properties of the environment. Should it be the case that the agent makes use of the signals from these virtual sensors, then we are at liberty to conceptualize that agent as engaging in a kind of primitive processing of internal symbols; that is, a kind of protorepresentational activity.

In painting a picture in which *representation* emerges naturally out of a primitive, constructive learning operation, the TFT model gets well away from the traditional, cognitivist approach that simply assumes representation to be a basic cognitive operation. It enables us to characterize the role that representation plays without importing the baggage of representationalist tradition—frames, databases, default hierarchies, symbol systems, and so on. It also frees the concept of representation from its links with symbolic artificial intelligence. The nuts and bolts of the TFT model are essentially algorithmic and computational. But the nature of the processes described is sufficiently primitive that they could easily be re-rendered in a connectionist or neural-networks paradigm.

11.9 Is TFT Nouvelle or Classical?

In recent years, cognitive science has been going through a period of upheaval. The traditional basis of the enterprise has been the digital computer and its utilization as a basic model of cognitive function. Cognitive theories have therefore tended to be strongly informed by concepts of algorithmic computation. But increasing numbers of researchers now question this bias. They point to the rather glaring differences that exist between the underlying hardware of the natural brain and that of the digital computer. They suggest that the manifest power and flexibility of digital processing have seduced the field into an overeager acceptance of cognitive models based on concepts of computation. The philosopher Timothy van Gelder, for example, argues that it makes more sense to try to understand the nature of cognition in terms of tightly coupled dynamic systems than in terms of digital computation.[2]

This rebellion against the computational foundation of cognitive science began in the 1980s and gathered momentum in the early 1990s. Robot researchers such as Rodney Brooks,[3] who had long complained that the emphasis on high-level tasks (such as chess playing) had led artificial intelligence (AI) to wrongly conceptualize cognitive function in terms of logical reasoning—computation by another name—found themselves bouncing along on the new, anti-tradition bandwagon. At the same time, the emerging field of artificial life (*ALife*)—which focused attention on primitive forms of simulated agency—and the work of researchers such as Randall Beer,[4] who focused on robotic insect models involving distributed models of computation—became integrated into the loose affiliation soon known as *nouvelle AI*.

Common to all nouvelle approaches is a *rejection* of the classical assumption that cognition is best understood as a form of computation (or symbol processing), and that representation and logical reasoning are therefore key. Researchers like Brooks stress the fact that mediating cognitive function via a central, logical processor operating in terms of representational constructs may impose a bottleneck on the system. A better way to proceed, it is proposed, involves utilization of relatively independent, reactive behavioral modules that are capable of producing effective action without reference being made to any underlying representational scheme. In Brooks's words, the world is its own best representation.[5] Thus agents may be able to get the effect of utilizing a representation of the world merely by modulating their interactions with it.

Classical researchers tend to take the view that this sort of non-representational approach may well succeed for simple behaviors but that it will not scale up. Nouvelle researchers, on the other hand, are quick to point out that classical, representation-oriented methods do not scale up either. The truth may be that while both paradigms have their problems, they both have something to offer, and that a nonpartisan approach is the one most likely to bear fruit. This is very much the line pursued by the philosopher Andy Clark. In a 1997 work,[6] he gathers evidence from a wide variety of sources to back the idea that natural cognitive function may incorporate both representational processes of the type envisaged by classical AI, and nonrepresentational processes of the type envisaged by nouvelle researchers.

The truth-from-trash model provides an image of learning and conceptual development that is very much in tune with Clark's integrative approach. It shows how efficient relational learning processes will tend to generate protorepresentational structures. But it does not impose any up-front commitment to the frames and knowledge bases of representationalist tradition. Rather, it demonstrates that we can invoke concepts of representation without importing the baggage of classical AI. It shows, in particular, that *abstraction* is possible without there being any commitment to the image of the "rational deliberator."

The TFT model also adds a wrinkle of fun to the concept of *embodiment*. According to the nouvelle canon, effective cognition requires genuine embodiment, that is, it requires that the cognizer be properly grounded in a nonsimulated environment. But the truth-from-trash model suggests that the key property in cognition is not the requirement for genuine embodiment but, rather, the requirement for an appropriate embodiment *profile*. Without the ability to undertake effective relational learning, an agent is not merely grounded; it is effectively *trapped* within its immediate sensory space. Its only recourse is the establishment of simple partitions within that space. But with the introduction of effective relational learning, the agent acquires the ability to escape its immediate embodiment—to interact with properties that are not explicitly manifest in the world to which it has direct sensory access.

The truth-from-trash model shows *how* this process may work. It shows the way in which agents may get access to abstract features of the environment by incrementally constructing a disembodied viewpoint on the basis of an embodied one. In some sense, it defuses the debate about embodiment by showing that the two opposed perspectives may be treated as special cases of something more general. It also eases the tension between computationalist and noncomputationalist positions within cognitive science. Many have argued strongly against the idea that conscious thought may be characterized in terms of computation.[7] But in the TFT picture, computation is made subservient to a characteristically non-algorithmic, trash-reorganizing process. Thus TFT offers us the prospect of eating our computational cake without having to suffer the bitter aftertaste.

11.10 Notes

1. Technically, we should refer to the "residual agent," that is, the part of the agent not actually engaged in the implementation of the virtual sensor.

2. van Gelder (1992).

3. See for example, Brooks (1991).

4. See, for example, Beer (1990).

5. Brooks (1991).

6. Clark (1997).

7. Roger Penrose (1989), for example, has swayed many with his thesis that there is "something non-algorithmic about our conscious thinking."

12

The Creativity Continuum

In this faculty of repeating and joining together its ideas, the mind has great power in varying and multiplying the objects of its thoughts infinitely beyond what sensation or reflection furnished it with.

John Locke[1]

12.1 Cincinnati Postscript

Following the debacle of Cincinnati's performance at the 1998 AAPC, the consortium of developers was quick to wash its hands of the poker project. Control then passed, by a circuitous process, into the hands of an obscure British researcher named Cedric Hooter. Hoping to retrieve something worthwhile from the wreckage, Hooter arranged for the Cincinnati hardware to be shipped from the AAPC site to his lab in Cambridge. He then turned his attention to the challenging issue of how Cincinnati could be transformed into the world-beating poker learner it was originally intended to be.

The system's lamentable performance was, as we saw in the previous chapter, the consequence of a fundamental design error by the development team. It chose to have the system use a card-based input language, and this irrevocably consigned the learning problem to the hard-to-penetrate relational camp. Hooter thus found himself faced with a choice of two possible "therapies." On the one hand, he could attempt to reconstitute Cincinnati's input language at a higher level of abstraction, thus providing himself with the leverage to eliminate the relationality of the learning problem. Or he could opt to integrate full relational-learning functionality into the system, thus enabling the problem to be solved as currently represented. It was pointed out to Hooter that the former strategy was likely to be the easier of the two. But he chose the latter, the choice being not quite as illogical as it seemed. Hooter harbored a long-term interest in the topic of relational learning, and he viewed the Cincinnati project as an ideal opportunity to explore his ideas more fully.

Hooter decided that as a preliminary exercise he should try to solve *by hand* the relational-learning problem faced by the defeated system. He therefore began experimenting with sample data from the main training set. To make his life easier, he constructed some simplified examples. In these, the inputs were constituted of specifications for a *single* hand and the outputs were numeric labels representing the *rank* of the hand. A small selection of these simplified examples is shown in figure 12.1.

Each row in this table represents an input/output pair. Each odd-numbered variable contains the face value for a particular card, represented as a number (where 10 = jack, 11 = queen, 12 = king, and 13 =

	x1	x2	x3	x4	x5	x6	x7	x8	x9	x10		x11
(1)	13	2	2	3	8	2	2	1	2	4	-->	4
(2)	8	3	6	4	6	2	8	3	8	1	-->	5
(3)	12	1	5	2	3	3	3	2	3	1	-->	4
(4)	13	4	13	3	8	2	8	1	8	3	-->	5
(5)	9	3	10	1	11	2	12	1	13	4	-->	7
(6)	10	4	10	3	1	3	1	4	10	2	-->	5
(7)	13	4	11	4	11	3	13	4	13	4	-->	5
(8)	9	2	4	2	5	2	13	2	10	2	-->	6
(9)	7	4	12	4	12	2	4	2	12	1	-->	4
(10)	13	2	8	2	1	3	1	3	1	4	-->	4
(11)	10	3	10	1	5	2	13	2	10	2	-->	4
(12)	13	4	3	4	4	1	3	4	3	4	-->	4
(13)	11	2	8	4	4	4	4	2	4	4	-->	4
(14)	11	3	11	4	13	1	13	1	13	3	-->	5
(15)	2	3	2	1	2	1	2	2	1	4	-->	9
(16)	8	2	2	2	9	2	11	2	13	2	-->	6

Figure 12.1
Simplified poker data

ace). The adjacent even-numbered variable holds the corresponding suit value (1 = hearts, 2 = spades, 3 = clubs, and 4 = diamonds). Values of the output variable represent the rank of the hand, using the following scheme.

```
1 Nothing
2 Two of a kind (a pair)
3 Two pairs
4 Three of a kind
5 Full house
6 Flush
7 Straight
8 straight flush
9 Four of a kind
10 Royal flush
```

Hooter's initial work involved experimenting with the different ways of applying the equality relationship to the data, much in the manner of a human BACON program (see chapter 8). As a first step, he considered measuring the equality of all ten input values. In the data at hand there are, in fact, no cases in which all the input values are identical. Thus the application evaluates to false in all cases. Hooter next tried applying the equality relationship across subsets of variables. This produced slightly more interesting results. Cases 8 and 16 turn out to exhibit equality among the same selection of variables. In fact, every even-numbered variable in both cases has the same value.

Hooter also investigated the possibilities of applying the equality relationship in a more flexible way. In particular, he tested to see whether there were cases in which arbitrary selections of *values* from particular data satisfy the relationship. This approach led to the discovery that cases 9, 10, 11, 12, and 13 contain at least three identical values, that is, three values which mutually satisfy the equality relationship. (He might also have discovered that in each case the relevant values come from the odd-numbered variables.)

Hooter's experiments with equality revealed that even using a single relationship in a single application protocol, there are typically many different results that can be produced. The operation of relational learning, he deduced, is a profoundly nondeterministic activity. The sorts of hand that may be "discovered" in the poker domain vary enormously, depending on the approach taken. A tendency to focus on equality relationships among specific variables tends to lead to the identification of effects corresponding to the existence of *flushes*, since in these cases the values exhibiting equality will always be sited in the same variables. A tendency to consider equality among arbitrary collections of values, on the other hand, leads more directly to the identification of *n-of-a-kind* hands.

In a recursive search process, such as implemented in TFT learning, the effects of the bias (i.e., the search strategy used) are cumulative. A bias that leads to the identification of flushes will—in the next round—lead to the identification of hands which are built out of flushes, such as *royal flushes*. A bias favoring *n*-of-a-kind hands, conversely, will tend to lead to the identification of hands that are built out of *n*-of-a-kind hands, such as *full houses*. The learner with one bias thus discovers one set of phenomena in the data, while the learner with a different bias finds a different set. In poker the possibilities are particularly numerous. A learner whose bias gave it a predisposition to consider integer *sequences*, for example, would be led to discover objects such as *straights* and *runs*.

From the practical point of view, Hooter took his results with the simplified poker data as indicative of the need to ensure Cincinnati was equipped with *exactly* the right bias. From the theoretical point of view, he took them as asserting something more fundamental about the subjective nature of learning. It was Hooter's impression that relational learners must always have a hand in the creation of their own sensory phenomena. He felt that to some degree they must necessarily create their own "worlds"—worlds that are necessarily constrained by the original data (or phenomena) but do not necessarily *reflect* them.

Hooter found the philosophical implications of this quite amusing. The argument implied that a relational learner has to be viewed as simultaneously "empiricist" and "rationalist", or at least as making some sort of transition from one mode to the other. In a typical relational-learning process, the original data (the raw phenomena) start out as the most influential factor. But as the learning proceeds, the accumulated consequences of the learner's own bias become increasingly dominant. There comes a point when the process has to be viewed as moving from a characteristically empiricist approach toward something more characteristically rationalistic. Eventually, the learner's influence on the process becomes paramount. The products of the "learning" are then primarily artifacts of the learner's own internal processes, marginally constrained by properties of the original data.

But Hooter was not a one for idle philosophical speculation. His real goal was more practical: to get Cincinnati to the point that it could (learn to) play a reasonable game of poker. And following his investigations with the simplified data, he was in a position to move immediately toward what he felt certain would be an effective solution. This involved obtaining a suitable relational-learning module and equipping it with the right bias (i.e., domain knowledge and search protocol). But before he proceeded to the logical conclusion of his investigations, he chose to pose one last question about the nature of relational learning. He asked himself what would happen in the poker domain if a given relational-learning process was allowed to continue *beyond* the point at which satisfactory performance is achieved.

Once again Hooter sought to establish the answer by experimenting on the data. But this time he did not curtail explorations at the point where the salient entities (runs, full houses, etc.) had been identified. Rather, he allowed the process to continue. The result, he found, was the generation of "imaginary" poker hands: weird "full houses" comprising three-card straights and two-card runs; strange "runs" involving ascending sequences of pairs; mind-boggling "flushes" involving alternating suits. And so on. The mechanical procedure he was applying was creating novel poker hands right before his eyes, the best of them combining a strong poker feel with a more zany, improvisational character. Metaphorical lightbulbs began to flicker on and off in Hooter's mind. Was it possible, he wondered, that a relational-learning process pushed beyond its natural limits would display a form of *creativity*?

Hooter's curiosity shifted into overdrive. The prospect of discovering a fundamental connection between the processes of learning and creativity hovered in his imagination, propelling him down an entirely new investigative avenue. Experiments were designed, performed, redesigned, re-performed, replicated and re-replicated. Results were tallied, tabulated, graphed, and analyzed in every possible variation. Finally, Hooter felt, there was no room left for uncertainty. Some sort of connection between learning and creativity undoubtedly existed. And relational learning of the "extended" variety was a reliable precursor of creative action. Relational learning, he concluded, should be thought of as a kind of cognitive nexus. Continued beyond the point of natural success, it would expand into an increasingly subjective realm, with the influence of raw phenomena gradually diminishing under the dominance of the process's own dynamics. Hooter dubbed the type of creativity generated in this way *relational creativity*.

Soon Hooter's original work on the Cincinnati system was forgotten while investigations into relational creativity occupied him day and night. His fascination with the idea of modeling creativity as "runaway learning" increased by the hour, and it was not long before he embarked on writing up his theory in the form of scientific paper. The beauty of the idea, he argued, was the way it handled the problem of *aesthetic appreciation*, that is, the feelings of pleasure and satisfaction which may be triggered by the process and products of creativity. According to Hooter's hypothesis, aesthetic pleasure could be viewed as the result of an evolutionary "piggyback." From the point of view of learning, he proposed, pleasure is a biological currency utilized in the implementation of positive reinforcement. Biologically speaking, then, relational learning is *expected* to generate pleasure, and the explanation of aesthetic pleasure follows straightforwardly: if creativity is associated with advantageous relational learning, creativity is naturally expected to generate feelings of pleasure. The aesthetic pleasure that is generated by the appreciation of artifacts created by *others* is, then, analogous to the feelings of pleasurable accomplishment generated through the acquisition of existing knowledge. Or so Hooter conjectured.

Ideally, creativity should be equated only with relational learning continued *beyond* the final point of agent advantage, Hooter conceded. But he claimed that this did not much affect the argument. In complex, real-world scenarios it is entirely plausible, he suggested, that positive reinforcement would depend as much on the form of the learning as it does on real-world consequences. In this case, reinforcement generation would not be able to "tell the difference" between relational learning logically within the creative category and relational learning logically outside it.

Hooter was thoroughly enthused with his new theory. In a flurry of activity he extended his paper to cover all aspects of his approach with respect to and in comparison with all known previous work on the topic. Unable to restrain himself, he submitted the paper to four journals simultaneously and then, without waiting for acknowledgment, set about writing letters of announcement to the quality newspapers. Hooter's aim in this was strictly philanthropic. He wished to raise awareness of the revolution in thinking about to be triggered by his paradigm-busting publication.

Unfortunately, the reviewers' comments, when Hooter eventually received them, were less than ecstatic. (Could the journals be using overlapping referee panels?) Comments were along the lines of "woefully ill-informed," "maverick," and "barking mad." All four journals rejected the paper. One editor was honest enough to state that the work should definitely not be published "in this or any other form."

Hooter, however, was unperturbed. He immediately set about a campaign of resubmission. This time he selected journals strictly at random and included in place of a covering letter a photocopy of the frontispiece of Johannes Kepler's magnum opus on Mars. This seemed to do the trick. Within a month he had received two acceptances. Very soon thereafter, his paper on relational creativity was in press.

From here, Hooter's rise was meteoric. In an appendix of his creativity paper he had included what he felt was a rather speculative commentary dealing with the relationship between *elaborative* and *pruning* processes in stable relational-learning regimes. Hooter proposed that the normal functioning of a relational learner depended crucially on there being a balance of power between the elaborative processes, which power the search, and the pruning processes, which keep it in check. He speculated that certain types of cognitive pathology might be comprehensible in terms of a breaking down in this balance of power, that is, a loss of equilibrium. Somewhat to his surprise, his proposal rang bells in the psychology community. He found himself thrust into the vanguard of research into causes of autism and other personal development disorders (PDDs). The result was a lucrative collaborative research proposal, the publication of a string of authoritative journal articles, and, eventually, the birth of a new paradigm: *Hooterism.*

12.2 Crash Landing at Gatwick

Standing in line, waiting to order hamburgers and fries for three, I notice a familiar shape reflected in the polished steel of the counter front. My three-year-old son has wandered over and is now standing next to me. Without turning around, I put out a hand and bring it lightly down on his shoulder. He asks me what I'm doing. "Getting some food," I say. The server arrives and nods expectantly. While reeling off my order, I extract four straws from the plastic dispenser and place them in my pocket. Then, just as the server finishes pushing the buttons on his cash register, I find myself thinking of bacon. Turning to my left, I see that the customer in the next line is about to return to his table with a tray full of paper-wrapped bacon burgers. "I want bacon," says my son. I call out to the server and point meaningfully toward the overhead menu. He shuffles reluctantly back. I start to say something about wanting to change one of the hamburgers for a bacon burger, but in midsentence I hear my name being called out over the PA. I stand and listen to the message. It occurs to me that we may not have time for burgers.

Although the events in this story happened several weeks ago, I can still remember them with perfect clarity. I can remember the bright fluorescent lighting of the airport terminal; the servers in their striped uniforms scurrying around between the shining machinery; the scraping of wooden-legged chairs on the tiled floor; the regular chiming of the PA; the smell of French fries, onion, and, of course, bacon; the feel of the fabric of my son's shirt; the sound of heavy luggage being yanked off a table. I can remember the whole environment surrounding the burger stand and in particular, the way it felt to be there.

But why do I recall these specific events in this specific way? Why should it be things like the PA that I remember? After all, when we get down to brass tacks, it is clear that *none* of the events I vividly recall actually "happened" to me. The sounds of luggage scraping did not happen to me. The PA announcement noise did not happen to me. The smell of bacon certainly did not happen to me. If we want to be strictly accurate, the only events that had a direct, physical impact on me were the sensory stimulations which took place while the story was unfolding. In the minute or so that I stood at the burger counter, zillions of photons traveling at the speed of light impacted my retinal surfaces. Vast numbers of airborne molecules made contact with the sensory cells in my olfactory system. Hundreds of differently textured surfaces came into contact with thousands of touch-sensitive cells on the surface of my body. Millions of tiny pressure waves pushed down into my auditory canals, producing a multitude of distinct sensory responses. But despite this overwhelming bombardment of phenomena, it is not the retinal, auditory, or olfactory stimulation that I recall. Instead, it is the PA, the plastic straws, and the bacon.

My memories of the events in the story are based ultimately on direct contacts made with submicroscopic objects such as photons and molecules. But that was *not* how it felt. My experience of the burger stand seemed just like any other experience. I had no awareness of processing sensory stimuli triggered by the arrival of photons and other objects. Rather, I felt myself to be seamlessly connected to the burger-stand environment. I did not feel myself to be engaging in the processing of sensation. I was simply aware of the events going on around me.

So powerful is this sensation of *awareness*, that mechanistic accounts of the sensory basis upon which it is *presumably* implemented seem almost ludicrously implausible. Can it really be the case that when I glanced down and gazed for just a second at the patch of fuzzy colors on the gleaming front of the counter, my visual system engaged in some sort of signal-processing extravaganza that had the ultimate consequence of convincing me my son had arrived at my side? When I look around, it does not feel as if I am rotating a sensory surface so as to intersect different photon bombardments. It feels as if I am *scanning* or *probing* my environment. It feels as if I am getting out into the environment. It feels as if I am, in effect, being there.

This, the seemingly magical phenomenon of human awareness, is blessed with a special name: *consciousness*. And it is a measure of the extraordinary strength of the sensation that the topic is the subject of extensive philosophical and scientific investigation. Consciousness has, of course, been pressed into service as the distinguishing hallmark of human intelligence, that is, the thing that supposedly can never be emulated by any sort of artificial device.[2] But approaches that attempt to separate consciousness from its mechanistic, cognitive basis—to make it something special, above and beyond any mere signal-processing activity—may be missing the point.

Human awareness (or consciousness) is directed toward macroscopic events and phenomena—PA systems, luggage, bacon, and so on—because it is these phenomena that, unlike photons, are salient for human existence. But the strength and seamlessness of the experience, the fact that we are barely aware which sensory modality is active in the sensing of any particular phenomenon, the extraordinary detail (e.g., the springiness of the straws) and penetration (e.g., the recognition of my son from a fuzzed-up reflection in the front of a metal counter)—these things are not telling us that consciousness is the work of magic; they are simply telling us that human cognition is exceedingly powerful. We experience the world in the form of a "unitary thread" of being because from the cognitive point of view, that is exactly what is required. As cognitive agents, subject to evolutionary pressure, we have no interest in the details of sensory processing. We want the big picture. We want to know *where* the bacon is; not *how* we know it.

This view of consciousness as a fundamentally cognitive phenomenon is compellingly pursued by Daniel Dennett in his book *Consciousness Explained*.[3] Dennett's view is that the human sensation of consciousness is essentially a "fake"—a pretense that is useful because of the way it glosses over signal-processing implementation details. He describes the way miscellaneous and characteristically "trashy" sources of information may be integrated so as to provide the familiar unitary thread of conscious experience.

Like Clark's integrative approach (see chapter 11), Dennett's line on consciousness ties in nicely with the truth-from-trash story. In TFT, as in Dennett's account, higher-level conceptual phenomena are deemed to be ultimately grounded in a relatively messy configuration of disparate information sources. The unitary character and apparent coherence of the higher-level phenomena are viewed as a kind of pretense or *virtual* construct, achieved through a complex system of recoding and filtering.

But TFT promises to provide a new twist on Dennett's story. As the not completely fictional story of Cedric Hooter reveals, relational learning involves an agent-side input that becomes stronger as learning continues. A point is eventually reached when it becomes meaningful to talk about the process engaging in a limited form of invention. TFT thus encourages us to view learning not just as a passive *discovery* operation, but rather as an active process involving *creativity* on the part of the learner.

Of course, we know from theoretical work in machine learning that *all* learning methods contribute some form of bias and thus engage in a degree of creativity. But in relational learning—particularly recursive relational learning (as implemented in TFT)—the effect is stronger. A recursive relational learner engages in an incremental process in which the results of one learning step serve as the basis for the next. The contribution of bias is then *cumulative*. The more recodings the learner assembles, the greater the input from the learner. Very high-level recodings are then substantially the creative artifacts of the learner's *own* processing. Lower-level recodings, on the other hand, may be viewed as more "objective" in the sense that their properties are more severely constrained by the source data.

Where does the phenomenon of consciousness fit into this picture? An appealing possibility is that consciousness may be visualized as a phenomenon at the *transition* between learning and creativity—a process that exists, somehow, at the outer fringe of relational learning, just prior to the "onset" of creativity. On this view, consciousness is really what we expected it to be all along—a state created when sensory and virtual sensory processes are turned inward upon themselves. But, on this view, the phenomenon cannot be assumed to be exclusively human. Rather, it looks to be a natural and expected feature of *any* cognitive mechanism able to engage in extended flights of relational learning, the degree or intensity of the sensation being essentially a function of the internal richness of the system rather than of its genetic or biological status.

12.3 Demise of the Career Scientist

Much of the present chapter has been devoted to storytelling, but a serious point is, hopefully, bubbling to the surface. Hooter's excesses notwithstanding, there is a coherent argument suggesting that the processes we refer to as consciousness and creativity have their roots in recursive relational learning. The implications run deep, particularly with respect to the link between creativity and learning. As noted in chapter 9, science itself can be treated as a form of communal learning. The assumption that the process is based on *objective* inquiry, already undermined by Hume's induction argument and Heisenberg's uncertainty principle, is now placed under renewed bombardment by the observation that relational-learning processes operate on what is, in effect, a *creativity continuum.*

On this view, it is wrong to treat science as a process whose only aim is to test and probe an independent reality. Rather, we should treat it as an enterprise that at least in part has the aim of creatively *inventing* reality. Of course, it is nothing new to stress the role of creativity and aesthetics in science. Many individuals have gone to great lengths to establish the point. The great physicist Paul Dirac, for example, noted the key role played by his sense of *beauty* in his "discovery" of the electron equation.[4]

More famous, perhaps, is the case of Einstein, who on numerous occasions went out of his way to mark the creative basis of scientific activity, and to emphasize the indivisible nature of creative and scientific activity. "All religions, arts and sciences are branches of the same tree" was one famous remark; "Imagination is more important than knowledge," another.[5] And in regard to his own scientific procedure, Einstein had few doubts. "When I examine myself and my methods of thought," he commented, "I come to the conclusion that the gift of fantasy has meant more to me than my talent for absorbing positive knowledge."[6]

Hooter's relational-creativity idea is thus no shiny-new, radical hypothesis. It is, rather, an echo of long-standing arguments with prestigious associations. But arguably it adds something interesting to them. It allows the "creativity emphasis" to be given a *theoretical* foundation. It promises a justification, written in dry, computational terms, which establishes that, in addition to being philosophically appealing, Einstein's position with respect to the creative dimension of science is *technically* correct.

Surely, as our understanding of learning—the basis of all knowledge—improves, there will be an increasing awareness of the duality of invention and discovery. Scientists will be increasingly tempted to come out of the dulled-down "observation closet." The scientific process might then mutate into something more interesting, throwing off its pretensions of dryness and objectivity, and trumpeting rather than concealing its artistic dimension. This New Science would nurture a new breed of practitioner —the "synergist," perhaps—whose aim would be the generation of interesting artifacts without regard to modality. It would develop new evaluative techniques sensitive to both explanatory and aesthetic power. And it would establish new institutions dedicated to the nurturing and exploitation of an open and productive state of mind.

But that, of course, is all in the future.

Or is it?

12.4 Stop Press

Last-minute reports are coming in of a disturbance at the 1998 SPWBA convention. According to a spokesperson, an intruder—an elderly male pushing a shopping cart—penetrated the tight security arrangements and gained access to the main conference hall. The incident came to an end when the intruder was arrested by police. Three delegates were later treated for shock and mild trauma.

Transcript

Guard: Er, excuse me sir. Could I see your ID?

Intruder: Why?

Guard: It's only conference delegates in the main hall, sir.

Intruder: As you wish. [proceeds]

Guard: Errmm, I'm afraid you can't go in there, sir. Unless you have an ID.

Intruder: My friend, I do not fully understand your language. But perhaps you can help me.

Guard: I'd be glad to, sir, if you'd just step this way.

Intruder: [digging around in the trolley] Ah. I seem to have lost it.

Guard: What's that, sir?

Intruder: I can't quite remember. But it was something important. Now let me see. [sets off toward the center of the hall]

Guard: [into radio] We have a problem in the main hall. Can I have some assist? [sets off, then backs up to collect the cart] Excuse me, sir!

Intruder: [stopping a passing delegate] Please, I need your help. Could you direct me to the gallery?

Delegate: Who's that, then? Is that what they're calling the Microsoft stand?

Intruder: I have a small construction that I am hoping to exhibit. But I seem to have got lost.

Guard: [arriving with cart] Is this gentleman causing you any trouble, sir?

Delegate: Well, you could put it like that. [confidentially] He's a Microsoft plant. It's some kind of disinformation campaign. They're all over.

Guard: [taken aback] Ah, OK. I didn't know. Is this on the level?

Delegate: No it's goddamn cheek. Someone's got to get it stopped.

Intruder: Why is this shiny steel everywhere? I find it blinding. Is it a new genre? I'm so behind, I wouldn't know.

Guard: [to Delegate] I'll check in and see what I can do. [raises radio to mouth]

Intruder: [taking radio from Guard] Is this operational or just decorative? I find these miniature images quite a giggle. Ha! [pushing buttons] Hello, hello. What? I don't know that, but yes, I do have a question, as it happens. [Guard showing signs of agitation] Could you tell me where you are placing exhibitors of aesthetically oriented work? What? Yes, I have something that I think may be of general interest. How much?

Boss: [hurrying to the rescue] OK, OK, fun's over. What's going on? Can I have a report, please? Just the facts.

Guard: I don't think there's a problem. This gentleman appears to be lost.

Intruder: No, this is not so. I dispute it. I am simply looking for somewhere to exhibit my work. You may not believe it, but I have here, in this shopping cart, a system that is guaranteed to intrigue the senses.

Boss: Are we talking drugs?

Delegate: No, it's bourbon. Can't you smell it?

Intruder: I may not be quite as imaginative as I once was. My mathematics is hopeless. Worse than a schoolchild. Mind you, it was never particularly good.

Guard: We have a whisper that it's a Microsoft stunt. They probably want us to make an arrest. Do we have the TV people in today?

Boss: I'm sorry, sir, we had the math geeks in last week. This is hi-tech now. If you're on the Microsoft team, I can escort you back to their stand.

Intruder: I'm not sure if I am or not. What sort of math do they like? I don't like these old-school scientists. They treat their work like sport. They just want to satisfy their ambitions.

Delegate: [suspicious] Why don't you tell us who you are?

Intruder: Sometimes I am this. Sometimes I am that. Today I am an artist who's feeling very proud of his work. All I want to do is find a small corner of your magnificent hall where I can set up my equipment. Is this an impossibility?

[*Boss,* *Guard* and *Delegate* exchange glances]

Boss: [turning away] I'm going to have to check this out on the computer. If this is a Gates stunt, I don't want us involved. Right? You got it?

Guard: No problem. [moves away and watches from a discreet distance]

Intruder: [to Delegate] Well, I guess that got rid of them!

Delegate: Who are you?

Intruder: Oh, my goodness, I forgot to introduce myself. By the way, I like these ... what are they, sculptures? [indicates tangle of wiring] But you should put them somewhere where people can see. If you get a chance, come along and look at my own work. I think it's my best ever. I'll be ... well ... somewhere over there, I should think. [moves off]

Guard: [talking quietly into his radio] The situation's deteriorating. We need more guys down here. I don't know, but he's walking around in circles, getting stuff out of the cart. Yeah, don't worry. If I see anything suspicious, I'll.... It just looks like, I don't know ... camping equipment, I reckon. Are we getting this on the tape? Video, too? No, I'm sure he can't. Hey, wait a minute, he's setting up some kind of billboard thing. Yeah, white. Quite large. You got it? He's trying to prop it up against the cart. No, I can't ... wait ... a minute ... I'll just move in a little closer. Right, OK, yeah, it's in English. OK. You got your pen ready? This is one for the books. It says "the machine that can learn anything."

Notes

1. From "Of Complex Ideas," in *An Essay Concerning Human Understanding*.

2. This line of argument is sometimes associated with Roger Penrose (1989).

3. Dennett (1991).

4. Noted by Penrose (1989), p. 545.

5. "What Life Means to Einstein: An Interview by George Sylvester Viereck," *Saturday Evening Post* (October 26, 1929).

6. This quotation taken from http://stripe.colorado.edu/judy/einstein/universe. html in April, 1998.

References

Beer, R. (1990). *Intelligence as Adaptive Behavior: An Experiment in Computational Neuroethology*. Academic Press.

Breiman, L., Friedman, J., Olshen, R. and Stone, C. (1984). *Classification and Regression Trees*. Wadsworth.

Brooks, R. (1991). Intelligence without representation. *Artificial Intelligence*, 47: 139–159.

Clark, A. (1997). *Being There: Putting Brain, Body and World Together Again*. MIT Press.

Cole, A. (ed.). (1969). *Numerical Taxonomy*. Academic Press.

Colville, J. (1985). *Fringes of Power—Downing Street Diaries 1939–1955*. Hodder.

Dennett, D. (1991). *Consciousness Explained*. Little, Brown.

Dietterich, T., London, B., Clarkson, K., and Dromey, G. (1982). Learning and inductive inference. In P. Cohen and E. Feigenbaum (eds.), *The Handbook of Artificial Intelligence*, vol III. Morgan Kaufmann.

Fahlman, S., and Lebiere, C. (1990). The cascade-correlation learning architecture. In D. S. Tovrezky (ed.), *Advances in Neural Information Processing Systems 2*. Morgan Kaufmann.

Feynman, R. (1985). *Surely You're Joking, Mr. Feynman: Adventures of a Curious Character*. Unwin.

Gibson, J. (1979). *The Ecological Approach to Visual Perception*. Houghton Mifflin.

Hendriks-Jansen, H. (1996). In praise of interactive emergence, or why explanations don't have to wait for implementations. In M. A. Boden (ed.), *The Philosophy of Artificial Life*. Oxford University Press.

Hodges, A. (1992). *Alan Turing: The Enigma of Intelligence*, Unwin.

Holte, R. (1993). Very simple classification rules perform well on most commonly used datasets. *Machine Learning*, 3: 63–91.

Koestler, A. (1959). *The Sleepwalkers*. Penguin.

Kohonen, T. (1984). Self-Organization and Associative Memory. Springer-Verlag.

Langley, P. (1978). BACON.1: A general discovery system. In *Proceedings of the Second National Conference of the Canadian Society for Computational Studies in Intelligence.*

Langley, P. (1979). Rediscovering physics with bacon-3. In *Proceedings of the Sixth International Joint Conference on Artificial Intelligence*, vol I. Morgan Kaufmann.

Langley, P., Bradshaw, G., and Simon, H. (1983). Rediscovering chemistry with the BACON system. In R. Michalski, J. Carbonell, and T. Mitchell (eds.), *Machine Learning: An Artificial Intelligence Approach.* Tioga.

Longmate, N. (1976). *Air Raid: The Bombing of Coventry, 1940.* Hutchinson.

Michie, D., Spiegelhalter, D., and Taylor, C. (eds.). (1994). *Machine Learning, Neural and Statistical Classification.* Ellis Horwood.

Minsky, M., and Papert, S. (1988). *Perceptrons: An Introduction to Computational Geometry* (expanded edition). MIT Press.

Muggleton, S. (ed.). (1992). *Inductive Logic Programming.* Academic Press.

Penrose, R. (1989). *The Emperor's New Mind: Concerning Computers, Minds, and the Laws of Physics.* Oxford University Press.

Rissanen, J. (1987). Minimum-description-length principle. *Encyclopedia of Statistical Sciences, 5.* Wiley.

Rumelhart, D., Hinton, G., and Williams, R. (1986). Learning representations by back-propagating errors. *Nature*, 323: 533–536.

Russell, B. (1912/1967). *The Problems of Philosophy.* Oxford University Press.

Schaffer, S. (1994). Making up discovery. In M. A. Boden (ed.), *Dimensions of Creativity.* MIT Press.

Shannon, C., and Weaver, W. (1949). *The Mathematical Theory of Information.* University of Illinois Press.

Thornton, C. (1989). *Concept Learning as Data Compression.* Doctoral thesis, University of Sussex, School of Cognitive Sciences.

Thornton, C. (1997). Separability is a learner's best friend. In J. A. Bullinaria, D. W. Glasspool, and G. Houghton (eds.), *Proceedings of the Fourth Neural Computation and Psychology Workshop: Connectionist Representations.* Springer-Verlag.

Thrun, S., Bala, J., Bloedorn, E., Bratko, I., Cestnik, B., Cheng, J., De Jong, K., Dzeroski, S., Fisher, D., Fahlman, S., Hamann, R., Kaufman, K., Keller, S., Kononenko, I., Kreuziger, J., Michalski, R., Mitchell, T., Pachowicz, P., Reich, Y., Vafaie, H., Van de Welde, W., Wenzel, W., Wnek, J., and Zhang, J. (1991). The MONK's problems—a performance comparison of different learning algorithms. CMU-CS-91-197. School of Computer Science, Carnegie-Mellon University.

Turing, A. (1950). Computing machinery and intelligence. *Mind*, no. 59: 433–460.

van Gelder, T. (1992). What might cognition be if not computation? Research Report 75. Cognitive Science, Indiana University (Indiana).

von Uexkull, J. (1957). A stroll through the worlds of animals and men. In P. H. Schiller and K. S. Lashley (eds.), *Instinctive Behavior: The Development of a Modern Concept*. International University Press.

Webb, B. (1994). Robotic experiments in cricket phonotaxis. In D. Cliff, P. Husbands, J. Meyer, and S. Wilson (eds.), *From Animals to Animats 3: Proceedings of the Third International Conference on the Simulation of Adaptive Behavior*. MIT Press.

Winterbotham, F. (1974). *The Ultra Secret*. Weidenfeld & Nicolson.

Wolpert, D. (1996a). The existence of a priori distinctions between learning algorithms. *Neural Computation*, 8, no. 7, pp. 1391–1420.

Wolpert, D. (1996b). The lack of a priori distinctions between learning algorithms. *Neural Computation*, 8, no. 7, pp. 1341–1390.

Index